About the Contributors

Iain Deas is Head of Planning and Senior Lecturer in Environment and Development at the University of Manchester, UK. His research interests focus on the dynamics of regionalism and regional policy and institutional change, evaluation of the impact of area-based urban regeneration initiatives, and the measurement of neighbourhood socio-economic circumstances in cities. He is co-director of the Centre for Urban Policy Studies and has undertaken numerous research projects for government departments in Britain, for research councils and local and regional economic development and regeneration agencies.

Jaime del Castillo Hermosa is Professor of Applied Economics at the University of the Basque Country and President of INFYDE (Information and Development), Spain. He has longstanding experience in the field of innovation and technology development such as in the design of territorial development strategies in regions affected by development problems. He is also an expert in the evaluation of public policies in a regional and local context, ranging from the evaluation of European Union Structural Funds, business aid schemes, urban regeneration actions and training policies to the analysis of the promotion of innovation and technological development. He has worked on several occasions for the European Union, OECD, Inter-American Development Bank and the United Nations as well as for regional and local governments in Spain, Portugal, France, Italy, Greece, Slovenia, Romania, Bulgaria, Mexico, Chile and Panama.

Mike Geddes is a Professorial Fellow in the Local Government Centre, Warwick Business School, University of Warwick, UK. His research interests include a number of aspects of public policy, ranging from local democracy and partnership to local economic development, public services, and poverty and social exclusion in the UK and Europe. He has led and participated in a number of large scale policy evaluation studies, including evaluations for the UK government of Local Strategic Partnerships and New Deal for Communities partnerships, and currently directs a national evaluation of Local Area Agreements and Local Strategic Partnerships for the Department for Communities and Local Government. He has contributed over a period of several years to the work of the OECD LEED

Programme. His publications include "Partnership Against Exclusion? Local Regeneration Strategies and Excluded Communities" and "Partnership and Social Exclusion in the European Union".

Silke Haarich is a regional planner, consultant and evaluator of regional development policies and projects. With a PhD in Applied Economics from the University of the Basque Country, she has worked in the Spanish consultancy INFYDE (Information and development) since 1998 in the area of regional development and competitiveness and policy and project evaluation. She participated in the design, management and evaluation of national and European Union Structural Fund and innovation policies in Spain, Slovenia, and Romania. Between 2006 and 2008 she lived and worked as a local economic development expert in Bolivia.

Paul Lawless is Professor of Urban Planning and Policy at the Centre for Regional Economic and Social Research at Sheffield Hallam University, UK. He has undertaken numerous evaluations of economic development and urban regeneration programmes funded by the European Union, the UK government, research council and research charities. He is currently the Director of a 10 year national evaluation funded by the UK government's Department of Communities and Local Government into the regeneration of 39 deprived English neighbourhoods: the New Deal for Communities Programme. The most recent overview of progress within the NDC Programme was published in 2007.

Neil MacCallum is one of Scotland's leading economists with over 20 years experience of applied economics. He has worked in the private and public sector, holding a number of senior posts including Head of Appraisal and Evaluation at Scottish Enterprise from 1996-2006, Head of Project Appraisal and Training at OffPAT, London, and, most recently, Head of Strategy and Policy with the Scottish Chambers of Commerce. He is an Expert Advisor to a number of international organisations including the OECD and European Union as well as a number of government ministries and consultancies in various countries. He now runs his own business, Neil MacCallum Associates, based in Glasgow, Scotland.

Jonathan Potter is a senior economist in the Centre for Entrepreneurship, SMEs and Local Development of the OECD. He is responsible for the OECD's methodology and capacity-building work on the evaluation of local economic and employment development policies and programmes. His activities include capacity-building seminars on evaluation approaches, the development of strategic evaluation frameworks for regional and local development for national, regional and local governments and development agencies and the collection, use and exchange of local development indicator and inventory information. He has recently published an OECD Framework for the Evaluation of SME and Entrepreneurship Policies and Programmes and a Monitoring and Evaluation Framework for Regional and Local Development in Latvia.

Brian Robson is co-director of the Centre for Urban Policy Studies and Emeritus Professor of Geography at the University of Manchester, UK. His research on urban policy evaluation for a variety of government departments, and for research councils and charitable trusts, has spawned eight books, over 100 articles and numerous reports on urban topics. He served as President of the Geography Section in the British Association for the Advancement of Science, President of the Institute of British Geographers, and Chairman of the Heads of Geography in British Universities. He was a working group member of Lord Rogers Urban Task Force and a member of the UK government's Urban Sounding Board. He was awarded the Founder's Gold Medal by the Royal Geographical Society for his work on urban policy in 2000.

Ville Valovirta works as Customer Manager at the VTT Technical Research Centre of Finland, with a focus on innovation policy and public sector management. His main research interests are related to science, technology and innovation policy, public policy evaluation, foresight, regional innovation, and knowledge-based policy-making. Prior to joining VTT he worked as a public policy consultant in the areas of policy analysis and evaluation, regional innovation strategies, R&D funding, and technology transfer programmes. He has contributed to several programme evaluations and published on evaluation methods and utilisation of evaluation studies and foresight.

Colin Wren is Professor of Applied Microeconomics in the Business School at the University of Newcastle upon Tyne, UK. He has published widely on evaluation in mainstream economics journals, focused on developing methodologies for the evaluation of the employment and other effects of regionally-based industrial incentive and enterprise programmes. He has undertaken evaluation for a large number of public agencies, recently sitting on the steering committee for the UK government evaluation of regional grants. He is currently co-editor of the Regional Studies journal and is a project leader for the UK ESRC Spatial Economics Research Centre.

Foreword

Successful local development strategies are built on evidence – on local development needs, attainable objectives, policy alternatives, expected impacts, achieved results, and the interventions that work and do not work. Only when on-the-ground knowledge of such questions is brought to bear in an ongoing process of strategy design, implementation and adjustment will local development policies and those who develop them make their full contribution to improving lives.

It is critical that evidence is integrated into the process of strategy building from the very outset and seen as a key input into the process of strategy development over time. The use of evidence should not be limited, as is often the case, to 'ex post' evaluations undertaken only after considerable policy effort has been made and when it may be impossible to resolve mistakes. Information from past evaluations is of course extremely useful in exploring what should be done in the future, but a whole range of further evidence is also needed for the development of forward-looking strategic visions and for ex ante policy decisions.

In this book, we examine how to gather and use evidence to build more successful local development strategies, strategies that will better accommodate local area needs, capitalise on local area potentials and bring together a range of local stakeholders. It sets out the principles of developing evidence-based local strategies and discusses how to deal with difficult issues where they arise. As such, it contributes to the efforts of the Organisation for Economic Co-operation and Development (OECD) to foster a culture of evaluation and evidence-based policy making in local development through the activities of its Local Economic and Employment Development (LEED) Programme.

The book focuses in particular on the major issues and principles involved in evidence-based strategy making rather than on the technical details, which are the subject of numerous evaluation manuals. It can therefore be used either alone, as an introduction to the issues and principles, or in conjunction with evaluation manuals, in order to go deeper in understanding the purposes and approaches behind evaluation and evidence-based strategy making.

The process of strategy building and evaluation is not one that can easily be developed simply through reading guidance and manuals, and although this book will certainly help, it is important to put evidence-based policy-making into practice, and hence engaging in a process of 'learning-by-doing'. The OECD LEED Programme therefore also offers a range of complementary capacity-building support to central and local government and development agency professionals, including training seminars, mentoring in commissioning or undertaking pilot evaluations and advice and guidance on creation and improvement of strategic evaluation frameworks, each time bringing in the many experiences of the partners in our international network.

In this way, we seek to promote a broader cultural change that will increase the impact of local development policies by bringing about an increased use of evidence as a fundamental tool for local strategy making. This culture change needs to involve not only evaluation and strategy specialists, but also a much wider range of policy makers, politicians and representatives of partner and civil society organisations. Indeed, there is great demand from local development actors for assistance and guidance on good practice in strategy development and how to best use the available tools and methods in varying local situations.

Changing cultural habits is a difficult task and it can only be achieved through continuous and long-term efforts. This book aims to support these efforts by providing a better understanding of why and how the use of evidence in local strategy making can increase success.

This book is intended for local development actors who systematically aim at achieving major changes through often small means. Proper use of evidence and evaluation may indeed make a difference in their efforts.

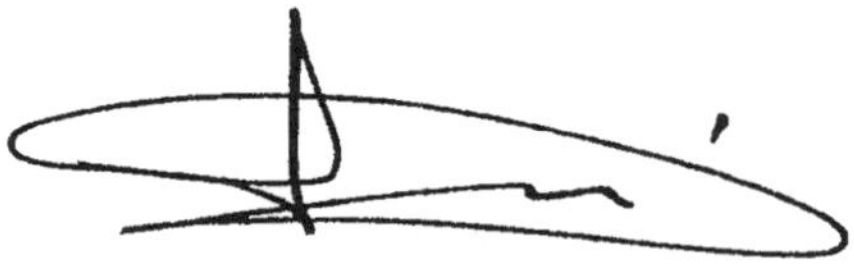

Sergio Arzeni
Director, Centre for Entrepreneurship,
SMEs and Local Development

ACKNOWLEDGEMENTS

This work has benefited from the support of the Unidea-UniCredit Foundation. Unidea-UniCredit Foundation is a non-profit foundation established by UniCredit Group. Among its initiatives, the Unidea-Unicredit Foundation offers support to those economic and social development projects which foster local development. Central, East and South East European countries represent one of the main geographic focus areas of the foundation's activities. For further information, please contact: Unidea-UniCredit Foundation, Via San Protaso 3, Milan, Italy, www.unicreditfoundation.org.

The publication was edited by Jonathan Potter, Senior Economist responsible for the evaluation work of the Local Economic and Employment Development (LEED) Programme in the Organisation for Economic Co-operation and Development (OECD). Very helpful support in the preparation of the publication was provided by Stefano Barbieri, Ivana Studena, Elisa Campestrin and Tina Bielawska of the OECD LEED Trento Centre for Local Development and by Lucy Clarke and Damian Garnys of the OECD LEED Programme in Paris.

We also acknowledge the contribution of the Autonomous Province of Trento in Italy, which provides financial and logistical support for the activities of the OECD LEED Trento Centre for Local Development.

Table of Contents

Executive Summary

Local economic development programmes too often fail to meet expectations because they are not based on a proper assessment of local needs and opportunities and lack a well thought out vision of how policy will make a difference. The appropriate use of monitoring and evaluation evidence in the design and delivery of local development strategies can rectify these failings.

Evidence on needs and objectives, policy alternatives and expected impacts can ensure from the beginning that the local development strategy is built on solid foundations. The evidence must of course be used systematically in the strategy building process and shared with all the relevant stakeholders, proper structures and processes for implementation of the strategy are required, and local actors also need a good information system that enables them to access the available evidence and to take it into account in their decisions.

The aim of this book is to show how to achieve this, and so to create and deliver more effective local development strategies based on the use of evidence. It discusses the major steps involved in evidence-based strategy building, the key principles to follow and the potential sources of problems and how to overcome them.

Each important step in the process of designing a strategy and assessing its quality is explained and examined, with a particular focus on the work that should be done in advance of implementation, involving making the key policy choices before resources are spent. Information is provided on *i)* defining objectives, *ii)* identifying options, *iii)* assessing expected impacts, *iv)* using strategic assessment results, *v)* implementing strategies and *vi)* developing information systems. Each chapter further contains a simple *Do's and Don'ts* schema, which offers an immediate checklist of the main recommendations to be acted upon.

Defining the strategic objectives

A first critical step in creating a successful local development strategy is the definition of clear and feasible strategic objectives. This in turn requires an understanding of how the local economy works. In particular it is important to:

- Understand how a wide range of social and economic factors interact. This can help to identify the specific barriers to growth that policy seeks to tackle and to avoid unforeseen adverse outcomes of interventions.
- Determine the most appropriate scales of intervention. The vertical links between regional, sub-regional and local processes of change mean that strategies at different scales need to fit together well and that the interventions chosen should be appropriate for the scale concerned by the strategy.
- Identify all relevant 'agents of change'. Effective partnership working can make a major contribution to the implementation of successful strategies, meaning that all the appropriate agencies should be involved in identifying and deciding priorities and hence in "owning" strategies.
- Identify the intended beneficiaries and how they should benefit from policy.

This whole process of defining strategic objectives, or what policy really wants to achieve locally and why, is at the heart of good strategy building and should be taken very seriously. A common problem, however, is that policy makers feel obliged to use what are seen to be 'best practice' or 'tried and trusted' approaches, rather than reflect on what could really make the difference in the particular conditions they encounter. For example, it is common for local actors to favour strategies based on the attraction of leading edge, high-tech companies – but in reality the extent to which this is a feasible option will vary considerably from place to place depending on the attractiveness of the location. In many cases other approaches may need to be considered that are both more feasible and more likely to make a major impact.

Identifying the options for intervention

Closely related to the creation of a set of strategic objectives on what policy should seek to achieve is the need to set out the main options for meeting these objectives. This is another common failing of local development strategies, namely that the alternatives are not properly considered before a preferred option is selected, so that potential opportunities may be missed and problems with the logic of the proposed intervention may not be uncovered until it is too late. For example, the option of a scheme to start up new companies in new sectors may be selected as the means to create jobs without reflecting on whether more jobs could be created through an alternative scheme for supporting firms in traditional sectors to upgrade.

A number of ground rules should therefore be adopted in identifying the options for intervention.

- The process of identifying options should be as transparent as possible and should involve reflecting backwards to defined objectives and forwards to anticipated impacts.
- In building up options, partners need to reflect on a range of criteria including the areas of intervention being addressed; the balance between harder physical investment projects as opposed to softer interventions associated with enhanced competitiveness; assumed beneficiaries; geographical scale; time horizons; financial and legal considerations; relevant actors and agencies needed for the effective implementation of options; appropriate management; and strategic steer and sustainability.
- Sometimes, in the short-run, doing nothing may be the better option and this should also be considered. This does not mean ignoring problems but waiting to act at the right time and when informed about all the possible implications, appropriate tools and suitable approaches available to fulfil the set objectives.
- In selecting the preferred option, partners will need to consider the degree to which options achieve defined objectives, the full anticipated costs and benefits of projects, and the risks associated with different options.

Assessing the expected impacts

A difficult but essential task for strategy building is to explore the expected impacts of the strategy and its various components. Assessing the likely impacts of different approaches and measures helps to assess which are likely to make the most difference and hence to make choices at the outset. Information on expected impacts also offers guidance on the advantages and potential difficulties involved with any measure. For example, it may become clear that the proposed action is at an insufficient scale to make the impacts on job creation or social exclusion that are expected. The collection of data on anticipated impacts and the setting of targets also adds legitimacy to the strategy building process as well as milestones against which progress can be measured and adjustments made to the strategy if progress is faster or slower than expected.

A key set of tasks is to identify the overarching questions to be addressed at programme-wide level, to specify what common information is needed and to establish the methods to collect such data. Overall, the choices will be made in relation to the objectives of the strategy and the purpose of the assessment being undertaken.

The approach taken will depend on several factors:

- The characteristics (nature, purpose, financial and geographical scale) of the development strategy, which determine its expected effects.
- The resources available to undertake the assessment (funds, time, data and human resources).
- The context in which the assessment is undertaken (economic, political and capacity and understanding of the user).

In measuring expected effects, it is possible to identify two main approaches. A top-down approach deals with effects at the aggregate level, for example for employment and output in industrial sectors or entire regions and localities, and focuses on the aggregate impact in relation to global objectives. A bottom-up approach deals with effects at the individual agent level, and focuses on outcomes at micro-level in relation to specific objectives.

Choices must also be made concerning assessment criteria, indicators and methodology. Assessment criteria are used for making judgements, such as those relating to efficiency or effectiveness. Indicators of outcomes and impacts need to be chosen, in relation to objectives. The choice of methodology involves decisions on data, techniques and tools that will form the basis for the analysis of impacts. In some cases this may simply mean setting benchmarks by which to judge the future performance of a strategy. In other instances it may involve sophisticated modelling of expected impacts. To some extent methods adopted will depend on the questions asked, and the nature and scale of the development strategy and the characteristics of the local area. Other key factors are the availability of data and the capacity of agencies both to carry out and to utilise emerging findings.

It is important not to overcomplicate the process and to use measures and techniques that are 'fit for purpose'. Many very sophisticated approaches are available, but often more basic 'rule of thumb' approaches are appropriate.

Making use of the strategic assessment results

To make a difference to the success of the strategy, the monitoring and evaluation evidence collected must be used. This may appear obvious, but a common problem is that evidence gathering is seen more as a technical exercise, aside from the real questions of decision-making and delivery, rather than as an integral part of the strategy making process itself. To the contrary, the use of evidence in strategy design and adjustment is crucial to bring about a more coherent local development strategy and increase collective learning about the means to attain set goals.

The following will help in ensuring that assessment results are fully used in the strategy making process:

- The commitment of various stakeholders to gathering and using evidence. This can be built through planning how and when stakeholders will use the results, planning how to communicate the results and mobilising political support around the integration of results in decision processes.
- The use of sound and valid evidence gathering methods with credibility and relevance.
- The involvement of local actors in data collection, analysis and reporting using a range of formal and informal social interaction processes amongst the various actors.
- The use of evaluation and appraisal methods that involve the participants and are aimed at having an impact on their thinking and behaviour.

Implementation of the local development strategy

Implementation is the crucial stage in bridging the gap between objectives and outcomes. It is therefore important to consider from the outset how implementation will be successfully achieved and what sort of obstacles to success may emerge. The following are at the heart of a good implementation process:

- Transparent delivery systems.
- Clear management methods and identification of responsibilities.
- Inclusive leadership, engaging the full range of partner organisations.

- Commitment from organisations and individuals to perform and deliver within agreed timescales and available resources.

Certain tools can be applied to ensure this happens. The most appropriate tools will depend on the local context, scale of the challenges being addressed in the strategy and the sophistication of partnership arrangements.

Setting up an information system

Information systems are the backbone of local development monitoring and evaluation systems. Setting up an information system starts with establishing what needs to be known in order to design a strategy that meets local needs and what needs to be measured over time to monitor how well the strategy is working. It is also necessary to decide how to collect, store and use this information and how to involve key partners and other stakeholders in the process.

A number of the principles for the development of information systems can be identified:

- Information systems should be designed to feed into key strategy assessment activities including needs assessments and baseline studies and monitoring of the financial, activity and impact performance of programmes over time.
- The information system should be capable of identifying problems promptly and anticipating potential problems so that corrective action can be taken to solve them.
- The information system should be seen as a means to end, namely supporting strategy design and delivery, and not as an end in itself. It is important to avoid creating overly technical systems that are difficult to access and manage or systems that are very expensive compared with the value that they provide.
- It may be more important to create a feasible and useful information system that facilitates basic data access and enables assessment of project activities, outputs, and outcomes, rather than having a comprehensive, but over-complex data storage system, without any corresponding capacity to analyse or understand data.

Each information system should be adapted to the different types of information required by its users and appropriate sources should be identified for each category of indicator or information required.

Introduction

Developing an Evidence Base: The Issues

by
Mike Geddes

The purpose of this book

The purpose of this book is to support a stronger culture of evaluation of local development policies and strategies. It provides a guide to principles and issues in using evaluation evidence in strategy development for policy makers and local development practitioners (including providers, users and commissioners of evaluation, locally, nationally, and in international institutions). It is intended to complement the various practical manuals already available (see the bibliography). While most OECD Member countries have introduced strong evaluation at the national level, including evaluation of their sub-national policies and programmes, it seems to be difficult to ensure that evaluation becomes an integral part of the strategy development process at the local level. The book is intended to help bridge this gap.

Our major focus is on the prior assessment stage of evaluation.[1] This reflects the fact that this stage of evaluation appears to receive the least attention and is most likely to be omitted when strategies are being developed and implemented at the local level. Factors that contribute to this may include:

- There may be little awareness of the benefits that prior assessment can bring, such as learning, improved strategy design, management and delivery.
- The capacity to undertake prior assessment may be insufficient at the local level.

- There may be a general hostility to evaluation, which tends to be perceived at the local level as a control tool employed by the national administration.

This book argues that effective development and use of evidence at the outset of designing local development strategies can identify problems and deficiencies, help to address such problems, and lay the basis for effective implementation and delivery. Such prior assessment is a starting point for a local development strategy that integrates evaluation as one of its key elements. Without this, individual projects and programmes risk losing their linkage to wider strategic goals, which in turn determine the long-term success of the local strategy. In this view a local development strategy based on sound prior assessment evidence has better prospects of achieving local development objectives.

This introductory chapter sets the context for evidence-based strategy building. The next section shows how local development strategies have become increasingly important but still face serious challenges. It is then argued that evaluation – and in particular prior assessment – can help overcome some of these problems, if a strategic approach to evaluation is adopted. The collection and use of evidence for strategy building, particularly at the prior assessment stage, is then discussed and its main components, which are addressed in subsequent chapters, are outlined. The remaining sections of this chapter consider issues concerning the commissioning of evaluation, including prior assessment, showing how some of the pitfalls sometimes associated with evaluation can be avoided if a local culture of evaluation and learning is built up.

Local development

There is increasing awareness of the important role of local development within wider national and supranational development strategies. Among the factors contributing to this "return of the local" are: the recognition of the importance of localised structures and processes in maximising the benefits and minimising the drawbacks of globalisation; the dynamism of local production systems; the need to pay more attention to social balance and to nurturing social capital; and an increasing awareness of the quality of job creation and skill retention resulting from locally integrated development trajectories.

In this understanding, the local dimension provides added value to more large-scale policies, and creates a robust grounding for long-term improvements in overall social and economic conditions. In financial and economic development terms, locally based activities and structures are becoming increasingly appreciated for their capacity to release the potential of previously overlooked or undervalued resources.

The local development process involves a range of strategic approaches, applications and frameworks that vary according to territorial scale and available resources. A useful way of describing the configuration of a local development process is by setting out its key components (OECD, 2001).

- **The driving role of local actors**. The mobilisation of local actors through local development initiatives helps to generate additional proposals for action and resources and competencies to help achieve them. Local development policies enable local actors to act as catalysts for development and draw on the ideas, energy and commitment of local people.
- **The knowledge of local assets and potential**. Local awareness of needs and opportunities and local involvement in strategy development helps to tailor policy solutions towards the distinct requirements of each area and provides feedback on the effectiveness of the actions that are undertaken. Thus local development policies adapt responses to local needs.
- **The enabling environment via local structures**. Local development structures provide a forum for an integrated approach to policy delivery in which various instruments and funding streams are combined for maximum effectiveness. This can lead to better co-ordination of policy, which is important given the multiple causes of unemployment, poverty and social exclusion for example.

The key mechanism of putting the concepts of local development into practice is that of a **local development strategy**. Local development strategies are now characteristic of all OECD countries (OECD, 2004).[2] Some are the result of purely local initiatives by municipalities or citizens, but many are initiated and supported by national or regional government policies and programmes. Local development strategies may be concerned with a wide range of issues: economic competitiveness and growth; employment and local labour market issues; local public services; environmentally sustainable development. Many are multidimensional, covering several of these domains. While most frequently local development strategies are concerned with the problems of lagging or deprived areas, they can also focus on issues such as the management of growth in prosperous towns, cities and regions. They can focus on the very local – a neighbourhood – or a wider area such as a city, a local labour market area or a region. Local development strategies are widely recognised as offering distinctive advantages, especially a close knowledge of local conditions and an ability to harness the contribution of local partners. Local development strategies provide a framework within which specific projects and funding sources can be utilised to the greatest advantage, thus creating a strong basis from which further funding can be attracted. They can also assist in the more effective delivery of regional and national programmes and policies.

However, while the widespread occurrence of local development strategies is testimony to their perceived value, it is also the case that such strategies frequently encounter **difficulties** and often are unable to deliver the outcomes and impact which are anticipated, either by local actors or by governments. These problems may reflect a number of factors, for example unforeseen changes in the economic environment in which the strategy is operating, or political and policy changes. But problems can also arise from deficiencies in the ways in which local development strategies are developed, managed and delivered. Too often, local strategies are generated too hastily, without sufficient consultation to ensure that key partners are "signed up" and without enough consideration of the range of strategic options and their strengths and weaknesses. If this is the case, a local strategy is all too likely to be ignored by partners as they proceed with their own priorities, or to be bypassed by events. If such problems are to be minimised, the need is for robust local strategies which consider a number of possible issues:

- Does the strategy show how local and national priorities will be met?
- Does it demonstrate clearly how delivery will be achieved?
- Is the strategy based on robust evidence?
- Are there plausible links between problems, objectives, actions, outputs and outcomes?
- Are partners, stakeholders, funders, citizens and communities "signed up"?
- Is the strategy achieving its objectives and delivering value for money?
- Are there mechanisms to review progress and adjust to change? (Neighbourhood Renewal Unit, 2006).

This book demonstrates that the use of evidence and evaluation – especially at the outset of strategy design and delivery – can be helpful to those facing these issues as part of the planning and managing of local development strategies. They can help both policy makers and practitioners at the local level, and those in national government responsible for the development and management of programmes delivered through local development projects and programmes.

The benefits of evaluation

Evaluation[3] can help local development programmes and projects to deliver by providing evidence on a number of issues:

- Identifying **what** works, **how** and **why,** in order to improve effectiveness. A key issue on which evaluation can offer objective evidence is "did it work?" Did a specific local development intervention deliver the intended outputs and outcomes? But further crucial questions for local development strategies concern how and why interventions succeed or fail. If they succeed, it is important to know the processes by which they worked, so that consideration may be given to whether a specific initiative can be mainstreamed and replicated elsewhere. If an intervention failed to deliver, it will be important to establish what exactly went wrong. Were the problems, for example, relatively superficial (in which case some fine-tuning may be the answer) or were they structural, meaning that this kind of intervention may need to be abandoned? Much of this is a question for later stages of evaluation, but it is also important to ask questions about the feasibility and robustness of different potential strategic objectives at an early stage.

- Identifying and understanding **problems** and **unintended consequences**. Local development strategies exist in complex and often fast changing environments. A local employment strategy may be faced by the sudden collapse of a vital local employer. Major social and demographic changes may occur, altering patterns of need. Evaluation which helps local development projects to understand, and possibly predict, changes in their environment, may help to mitigate the consequences of such problems. But a further issue is that policy interventions may have not only planned, but also unanticipated outcomes and impacts. Thus an intervention designed to benefit one neighbourhood may merely shift some problems to adjacent neighbourhoods. Interventions to upgrade skill levels may not improve the skill base of the locality if those who have acquired the skills move away. Good evaluation can again give policy makers and practitioners greater awareness of such unintended consequences. Again, prior assessment should initiate an approach to evaluation – for example by developing alternative scenarios as part of the process of identifying strategic priorities – which seeks to highlight problems and unintended consequences.

- **Accounting** for how resources have been used and demonstrating **value for money**. A common question – which too many local development projects find it difficult to answer – is "where has the money gone?" A basic function of evaluation is to track resource utilisation. However, if knowing where the money has gone is the first issue, then being able to demonstrate it has been well spent is the second issue. Evaluation can contribute to identifying value for money by assessing the effectiveness and efficiency of resource utilisation. Prior assessment has an important role in this respect in evaluating strategic alternatives in terms of the optimum use of resources.

- **Involving** and **accounting** to **stakeholders** (partners, funders, politicians and local people). Evaluation provides policy makers and practitioners with evidence about the performance of local development interventions. Too often, this is regarded as "technical" information, and is not shared beyond a small circle of those involved in the initiative. But evaluation can also, in a positive cultural climate, serve to enhance involvement and accountability in local development strategies. In the first place, an assessment of strategic options should involve stakeholders in the local development process by seeking their views on a range of issues. Secondly, sharing the results of evaluation with stakeholders – from funders to local people, can greatly improve the level of understanding of what a project is achieving over time. Even when evaluation highlights problems, it can help stakeholders to understand why problems have developed – and engage them in finding solutions. In short, one of the benefits of evaluation can be to turn stakeholders who may potentially be "outsiders" into "insiders".

There are thus a number of potential benefits from evaluation. Some of these are likely to be more important than others, depending on the nature of the local development strategy. What is important, though, is for consideration to be given at the outset to the purposes and benefits which evaluation and evidence gathering is intended to deliver, and then to design an evaluation strategy accordingly.

Components of an evaluation strategy

A robust evaluation strategy will involve a combination of formative and summative, *ex post*, mid-term/*in itinere* and *ex ante* elements.

Evaluation can be of two broad types, formative and summative:

- Summative evaluation is concerned with **results**. Within a wider evaluation framework, summative evaluation tends to be more important towards the end of the life of a local development strategy, when the question of outcomes is crucial.

- In contrast, formative evaluation is more concerned with **processes**. As the term suggests, the primary purpose of formative evaluation is to help **form** the strategy and its delivery as they develop. It is thus of major importance in the early period of operation of a local development strategy. Within a strategic approach to evaluation, a prior assessment of the evidence on needs and opportunities should be regarded as the key initial component of formative evaluation. While formative evaluation is often only commissioned once a local strategy has been adopted, the essence of prior assessment is to help "form" the strategy at the pre-adoption stage, before key decisions about strategic orientations have been made.

  Thus **formative evaluation** is often concerned with questions such as:

- How effective are the structures and working practices through which the local development strategy is developed and delivered? Are there effective processes for stakeholder engagement? Does the project team have, or have access to, the skills it needs? Are partnership relationships supportive of the strategy? Do other similar initiatives suggest ways in which the local strategy might be delivered more effectively?

- As the process of implementing the strategy proceeds, are interventions and projects and also resource deployment contributing to the agreed targets and to strategic objectives? Are there any changes in the external environment which need to be considered? Do the initial objectives and targets remain valid, or does experience suggest some modification of the initial strategy?

Prior assessment is crucial to formative evaluation in that it provides a robust baseline from which progress can be judged. Information about local trends, needs, potentials and problems which will be gathered during the prior assessment stage should constitute an in-depth assessment of the local area prior to the inception of the strategy. This evidence helps ensure that the strategy is well grounded and that it can then inform ongoing monitoring and performance management.

Formative evaluation requires the evaluator to be seen as the "critical friend" of the initiative, offering both praise at what is going well, but not afraid to say when things need changing. Formative evaluation is likely to depend significantly on qualitative data. It is likely to involve gathering evidence from those responsible for the delivery of the strategy, and from partners and stakeholders, and from communities and citizen groups, especially those who are the proposed beneficiaries of the strategy, about progress and about possible barriers to success which need to be overcome. It requires a close and trust-based relationship between the evaluation team and those implementing the local strategy. This will allow the evaluation to "dig deep" in understanding how the strategy is working, and for those responsible for the strategy to take on board formative evaluation findings. These may well include messages for national governments concerning the way local development programmes are managed, as well as for policy makers and practitioners at the local level.

The purpose of **summative evaluation** is to provide an objective picture of the outcomes and impacts of a local development strategy. There is sometimes a view that summative evaluation can be undertaken *ex post*, but it will be much more effective if a summative evaluation methodology is established as part of the prior assessment process and is in place throughout the life of a project. This will, in the first place, ensure that data collection is well organised from the outset – there are too many examples of *ex post* evaluations which have encountered problems because the necessary data is just not available. Secondly, an ongoing approach to summative evaluation can help assess outcomes and impacts during the life of the strategy, thus providing evidence upon which to adjust delivery if emerging outcomes are not satisfactory, or amend objectives and targets of the strategy if it becomes clear that these were not robustly specified in the first place, or if changing circumstances dictate that they need to be reconsidered. Problems which can arise may include:

- Un-ambitious or overambitious targets.
- Poorly specified targets.
- Too many targets and performance indicators.
- Limited relationship between problems, interventions and desired outcomes.
- A misfit between the priorities of the strategy and the allocation of resources.

Summative evaluation depends on a robust framework of baselines, targets, performance measures and indicators.

- **Baseline** – the starting point of existing conditions which the local development strategy aims to alter and against which subsequent activities and achievements must be assessed.
- **Objectives and targets** – the aspirations and objectives for local development set out in the strategy and the specification of them quantitatively and qualitatively. For example, an objective is frequently to lower the rate of unemployment, and this would lead to a target to

reduce unemployment by a defined amount during the period of implementation of the strategy.

- **Outputs** – the direct results of activity generated by the application of resources by the strategy. Examples related to the reduction of unemployment would include jobs created, training and skills enhanced, new business start-ups assisted, etc.
- **Indicators** – the set of quantitative and qualitative indicators which are used to measure progress and achievements against objectives and targets. Indicators of unemployment would include numbers and percentages of working age people on out-of-work benefits, if possible disaggregated by gender, age, geographical location, etc; numbers in employment, etc.
- **Outcomes** – the longer term changes in socio-economic or physical conditions which are due to the local development strategy. In relation to unemployment, this would mean assessing the extent to which changes in levels of unemployment could be shown to derive from actions undertaken as part of the strategy

Summative evaluation is thus centrally concerned with how resources are applied; whether outcomes and impacts are achieved and benefits accrue to the intended beneficiaries; whether interventions deliver value for money; and also with questions such as which elements of a local development strategy can be replicated (locally or in other localities) and, if the programme is coming to an end, what the lessons are for future policy and subsequent interventions. A benefit of a good prior assessment will be to ensure that the crucial questions for summative evaluation about the objectives and desired outcomes of the local development strategy, and how these relate to the "baseline" of local needs and opportunities, have been considered at an early stage.

Evidence for strategy making

The major focus of this book is on the use of evidence to design effective strategies from the outset, involving a process of prior assessment which supports the preparation of proposals for local development interventions. The purpose of prior assessment is to gather information and carry out analyses that:

- Help to define **objectives**.
- Ensure that these objectives are **feasible**.
- Instruments used are **cost effective**.

- Subsequent evaluation will be **robust**.

Prior assessment offers a number of benefits in that it can help:

- Identify **gaps** in a local development strategy, help to fill them, and show how this will help to deliver better outcomes.
- Question **fixed ideas** which local stakeholders may have, by exploring alternative possibilities in an evidence-based way.
- Create **linkages** between individual projects and programmes on the one hand, and wider strategic goals on the other.
- Ensure that local priorities are consistent with national policies.
- Ensure that evaluation does not become a formal exercise **imposed** by the central administration or sponsor.
- Avoid commissioning the evaluation process **in haste,** rather enabling it to be built into programme and project design from the beginning.
- Support a **bottom-up** approach to strategy development which may prove more successful in identifying resources and enablers for endogenous growth.

A serious prior assessment approach is likely to contain a number of components:

1. Defining strategic objectives.
2. Identifying the options for intervention.
3. Assessing expected impacts.
4. Making use of the results.
5. Establishing the framework for intervention.
6. Setting up an information system.

Each of these six components is discussed in subsequent chapters.

Commissioning evaluation

Local development organisations have a number of options when it comes to deciding who should undertake the evaluation that will provide evidence at prior assessment and subsequent stages. Each option will have advantages and disadvantages.

In the first place, there is a choice between doing evaluation in house or commissioning an external evaluator. This will be partly a matter of skills –

are there evaluation skills available within the project or within one of the major partners? In many cases, such skills are often in short supply as evaluation is a relatively specialised activity. However, if a local organisation wants to conduct extensive evaluation, there may well be a real choice between hiring external consultants and using the money to employ – or up-skill – project staff. There is much to be said for creating evaluation capacity at the local level. Evaluation undertaken within a local development agency can, at the very least, permit useful self-evaluation as part of a wider evaluation strategy. If the decision is made to do evaluation in house, then it is important to ensure that the internal evaluation team has sufficient autonomy for it to be able to present findings which may be challenging, while at the same time having sufficient status to ensure that findings are acted upon.

If the decision is made to commission an evaluation externally then the kind of choices most frequently faced are whether to choose consultants or academics, and whether to favour local or nationally/internationally respected experts. This will partly boil down to a question of cost, but there are other considerations. Consultants may be more expert than academics in working with practitioners, but may perhaps sometimes be less rigorous methodologically. Local experts may offer a greater familiarity with the local context of the strategy, but have less knowledge of best practice elsewhere. However, such "typecasting" is simplistic, and the real advice is that all the feasible options should be considered in commissioning the evaluation. This emphasises the importance of good practice in commissioning. A robust commissioning process is likely to involve:

- A clear and well thought through specification of the evaluation required. This needs to be sufficiently detailed to ensure that key outputs are delivered, but with sufficient flexibility to allow the evaluator to exercise their expertise. One important issue in developing the evaluation specification is whether the evaluators are asked not only to assess the progress of the strategy, but also to discuss the policy implications arising from their findings.
- A wide scan of possible options – in-house or external; consultants or academics; local or not, to arrive at a list of potential suppliers. One possibility may be to split the work between in-house and external providers, or between different external sources. This can offer real benefits, but the split will need to be clearly delineated to ensure positive synergy between the parties.
- A competitive and well-designed tendering process designed to assess the strengths and weaknesses of alternative suppliers, on the basis of

both costed proposals to the evaluation specification, and also an assessment of relevant previous work.

- In all likelihood, a process of negotiation with the preferred supplier to fine-tune their proposal in order to ensure it meets the needs of the project in full.

Once a provider is commissioned, attention needs to be paid to the ongoing relationship between the commissioning agency and the evaluation team. Best results are unlikely if there is little contact with the evaluators while the work is being done – or indeed at the opposite end of the spectrum if there is any attempt to micro-manage the evaluation on the part of the commissioning agency. The desirable middle ground is to create an active **partnership** between commissioners and evaluators, on a **relational contracting** basis.

These issues are common to many types of evaluation. But there are also issues which tend to impact more specifically on the evaluation of local development projects. One of these concerns the involvement of local people. In more traditional approaches to evaluation, local people would normally be regarded as one of the **objects** of evaluation. This prioritises questions such as whether the objectives of the strategy are specified in a way which reflects local needs, and whether these needs are being met through project outputs. But, in a similar way to that in which citizens and citizens' groups are now likely to be actively involved in local development strategies, rather than merely being the external beneficiaries of them, there is a growing recognition of the potential benefits of involving local people in evaluation (New Economics Foundation, 2000). This can take a number of forms:

- Local citizen participation in managing evaluation projects, for example as part of "oversight committees".
- Involvement of citizen groups and community activists in specific elements of the evaluation, such as undertaking local surveys.
- Training of local people to play a wider role in evaluation, thus combining their local knowledge and experience with more expert, technical skills.

The involvement of local people in evaluation needs to be carefully managed. But it can have a number of benefits, including widening the sense of local ownership of the evaluation, and providing people with new skills.

Finally, there is growing interest in forms of evaluation undertaken neither in house nor by external contracting but within **networks**. Networks of local development agencies or partnerships are now commonly seen as an important way of sharing experience of local development issues. These may be local, national, or cross-national. Some of these networks have developed **peer review** processes, in which the activities of each agency or partnership is reviewed by their peers in the network. If the peer review process is robustly constructed, this can prove to be a cost-effective approach to evaluation, which may be particularly useful in comparing the performance of local development initiatives operating in different contexts.

Problems of evaluation – and how to manage them

Despite the benefits it can offer, evaluation is often viewed as something to be tolerated rather than encouraged. It can often prove peripheral rather than central to local development strategy making. This is as true of prior assessment as it is of later phases of evaluation. There are several reasons for this:

- **Hostility**. Many local development agencies are small institutions tackling large problems. This can sometimes generate a "siege mentality" in which the last thing the agency thinks it needs is forensic examination by outside evaluators. Busy practitioners are often reluctant to find time for discussions, or to assist in data gathering and monitoring.
- **Bad news**. Evaluators can be the bearers of bad news. Local development projects are often the subject of argument and contention, and those committed to them may not want to hear that some aspects of the strategy are not working well.
- **Cost**. Good evaluation comes with a price tag. For local development projects which seldom have sufficient resources to deliver their own objectives, evaluation can seem a luxury. In the longer term, however, evaluation may well save money if it can demonstrate where value for money is or is not being achieved.
- **Shortage of time**. This is often a major issue at the prior assessment stage, when there can be strong pressures to move strategies into implementation mode. This can mean, however, that the foundations of the strategy are weak because of the lack of effective prior assessment.
- **Does it deliver?** Often, scepticism about evaluation relates to a concern that it will not deliver evidence which policy makers and practitioners need.

These are real and understandable concerns. However, if local development projects are genuinely interested in outcomes and knowledge of "what works", then evaluation – which can provide these – is essential.

The question therefore is how to manage these problems. There are several ways of ensuring that the potential of evaluation is realised.[4]

- **Involving people**. It is important that as many people as possible have a stake in the evaluation. Thus it may well make sense to identify one individual in the project team who is seen as the "champion" of evaluation; however it can then be problematic if everyone else regards evaluation as none of their business.
- **Demonstrating benefits**. The benefits of evaluation should be publicised. Too often, the capacity of evaluation to provide objective, expert validation of the achievements of local development strategies is not maximised.
- **Careful choice of methods**. It is crucial that the evaluation specification is well thought out, to ensure that it does what is needed.
- **A learning culture**. The reception given to evaluation will be conditioned by the organisational culture of the local development agency. Evaluation will be welcomed if that culture is a learning culture, in which a focus on delivery is balanced by a recognition that even for the most experienced professionals, there is still much to learn, and that agencies pride themselves on their openness to challenges and new ideas.

A culture of evaluation and learning

Evaluation evidence must not – as unfortunately it often is – be an afterthought or an add-on, commissioned in haste when things start to go wrong. Rather it should be built into programme and project design from the beginning. If there is a serious concern with outcomes – "what matters is what works" – it is essential to have proper evidence of what is working well in local development strategies and what fits with needs. A culture of evaluation means that there is real ownership of the concept and practice of evaluation, not just on the part of those directly responsible for undertaking evaluations, but also within policy and practitioner communities.

In the European Union, an evaluation culture is beginning to grow up because of the European Commission's need to maintain an overview of programmes and projects being implemented across many member states. In the United Kingdom, the election in 1997 of a government committed to "evidence-based policy making" (Nutley, Walter and Davies, 2003), has greatly enhanced the profile of evaluation. However, in both these cases, the commitment to evaluation is primarily driven from the top, by the Commission and by the UK government. This book makes the case for an evaluation and learning culture to be embedded at the local level as well, and sets out the major steps in using evidence to make local strategies work.

Notes

1. The concept of prior assessment has much in common with the *ex ante* evaluation associated with many EU programmes.
2. The OECD LEED Programme (Local Economic and Employment Development) has championed the cause of local development over many years. Through a critically supportive engagement with policy and practice in many OECD countries, the LEED Programme has been a powerful force for the identification and dissemination of innovation and good practice.
3. It is important to distinguish between monitoring, evaluation and performance management. An effective monitoring system is essential as the basis for evaluation and performance management. Evaluation is the process which uses the data provided by monitoring arrangements to critically assess the progress, outcomes and impact of a local development strategy. Performance management then applies monitoring data and evaluation findings to manage the delivery of the strategy.
4. These issues are treated in more depth in Chapter 4.

References

Neighbourhood Renewal Unit (2006), "Performance Management Framework: The NRU Model", Office of the Deputy Prime Minister, London.

New Economics Foundation (2000), "Prove It! Measuring the Effect of Neighbourhood Renewal on Local People", Groundwork and NEF, London.

Nutley, S., I. Walter and H. Davies (2003), "From Knowing to Doing: A Framework for Understanding the Evidence-into-Practice Agenda", *Evaluation* 9 (2), pp. 125-148.

OECD (2001), *Local Partnerships for Better Governance*, OECD, Paris.

OECD (2004), *New Forms of Governance for Economic Development*, OECD, Paris.

Chapter 1

Defining the Objectives of Local Development Strategies

by
Brian Robson and Iain Deas

Defining the objectives of a local development strategy is the initial step of a prior assessment process. Defining the right and feasible objectives requires an understanding of how local economies work and how they are connected with processes that operate at different spatial scales. In identifying the objectives for local economic development, it is crucial:

- To understand the complex interplay between a wide range of social and economic factors. This can help to isolate the specific barriers to growth and help to avoid creating unforeseen outcomes of interventions.
- To determine the most appropriate scales of intervention. The vertical links between regional, sub-regional and local processes of change mean that strategies need to fit well together, that different interventions may be appropriate at different spatial scales and that strategy and implementation may best apply at different scales.
- To establish links between the priorities and objectives at different spatial scales to avoid conflicts across the vertical levels of strategy development.
- To identify and include all relevant agents of change. Effective partnership working is essential for the implementation of strategies and this puts emphasis on ensuring that all the appropriate agencies are involved and can contribute to the process of identifying priorities and hence in "owning" the strategies.
- To identify the intended beneficiaries and ensure that maximum benefit is targeted at them.
- To consider the durability of outcomes in order to avoid the problems that too many interventions have only short-term benefits.

Introduction

The ultimate objective of any local development strategy must be to overcome the weaknesses and build on potential strengths of target areas. Well-defined objectives need to prompt focused efforts to create, maintain and/or improve economic and social conditions of a location, whether for an underperforming area or for an already steadily growing local economy.

In considering what may be the most appropriate objectives for local development strategies and interventions, policy makers and practitioners participating to the process face two main questions:

1. Understanding the origin and nature of the economic challenges confronting such areas.
2. Considering the types of intervention that might be most relevant.

Gaining agreement about objectives is a process that requires, but does not always receive, considerable attention, reflecting a number of obstacles:

- The situation is often complex and this leads to the impression that it is too difficult to determine priorities.
- Strategies may conflict across different agencies or spatial scales.
- Residents and/or businesses may have different priorities.
- It is difficult to get the private sector on board.
- It may be perceived that the strategy can only tackle the supply-side issues – the market determines demand.
- Monitoring and evaluation are considered as unnecessary and premature and the whole exercise as too bureaucratic.
- There is no clear understanding of the need for a specific development strategy when the local area is already prosperous.

This chapter will address some of these issues and show which activities are important in arriving at appropriate objectives. Some of the responses to the list of the obstacles may include:

- Thinking about how best policy could maintain or accelerate growth. Considering whether all sub-areas are equally competitive, and how strategy could help to harness untapped potential to advance growth and spread development.
- Developing a model of area-based change, using an appropriate conceptual framework, *e.g.* "theories of change".

- Developing vertical links through partnerships with the relevant agencies.
- Establishing a public agencies forum to sensitise stakeholders to the varying goals and to develop shared "visions" for the future.
- Developing a consultation process to explore views and seek compromises.
- Ensuring that meetings are task-oriented rather than talking shops. Seeking to engage a high-profile private sector person as board chair or member.
- Considering how to influence the supply chains of businesses so that greater local procurement can generate employment.
- Establishing as full a baseline as possible to help track change and identify future impact and effectiveness. Using the baseline to gain a better understanding of current problems and potentials and to inform the development of objectives for the strategy.
- Establishing monitoring and evaluation objectives that will be of genuine use in helping to refine the strategy in future. Convincing stakeholders of the real potential of monitoring and evaluation to be more than just bureaucratic "bean counting".

Understanding local economic performance

The crucial element in assessing the delivery potential of local development strategies is to understand the specific causes of an area's performance. If we can acquire a better understanding of the nature of local economies, this can provide the basis for deciding the specific objectives that may be most appropriate for any local development strategy.

Often, this task of characterising an area's balance sheet of assets and liabilities is approached in terms of some form of SWOT analysis – specifying the strengths, weaknesses, opportunities and threats faced by an area. This can be a helpful exercise in thinking through what should be the prime objectives of policy and in considering what is feasible in terms of future economic development. This can be useful because it moves the policy agenda away from simplistic conceptions which aim to address problems but which ignore potentials within an area. Linking the two – and ensuring that local economies capitalise upon potential areas of growth as well as addressing problems of under-performance – can be an important element of development strategies.

Using SWOT approaches to define objectives for local development strategies is helped by thinking systematically about an area's economic problems and opportunities in relation to a set of demand factors and/or supply factors. The elements in which an area may be deficient will clearly help to guide the choice of objectives for policy intervention.

The mix of economic activity

An area may develop economic problems because it has a high proportion of activity concentrated in sectors that are declining nationally or that have low productivity. This is frequently the case with old industrial areas which have an inherited legacy of, for example, textile factories or shipbuilding or coal mining or other activities which may no longer be as viable in a world of intensifying global competition. It may equally be true of other areas dominated by sectors that are no longer attuned to patterns of contemporary consumption. Seaside resorts in many northern European countries are a case in point: they had a strong economic rationale when large numbers of people took holidays within their own countries, but now that the holiday and tourist markets are global, places that lack reliable sunshine or the lure of the exotic face uncertain futures. The same can be true for some types of rural area, where agricultural restructuring may have generated surpluses of marginal or unproductive land, the future uses of which are uncertain, especially in the absence of subsidy of some kind. Equally, for many smaller towns, villages and rural areas, increased mobility and competition from multinational corporations in larger settlements have put at risk small shops, post offices and many of the traditional privately owned local service outlets.

One approach to better understanding the economic needs of areas is the use of shift-share analysis. This, with appropriate advice and help in the first instance, can provide an easily used tool to enable local practitioners to look at economic performance by partitioning growth into two main components:

1. A "proportional" component which is the outcome of the mix of activity in an area (so that places with a high proportion of low-performing activities nationally or regionally would be expected, other things being equal, to have lower rates of growth).
2. A "differential" component which measures the performance of an area, holding its sectoral mix constant, to see whether it over-performs or under-performs when measured against the regional or national performance of the same mix of activities.

Use of this shift-share technique can be a powerful way of identifying whether the economic characteristics of an area are the result of poor performance (and hence suggest a need to boost productivity through, for example, investment in plants and machinery, higher skill levels, greater product or process innovation or more effective marketing); or alternatively are the result of the inherited mix of activity (and hence suggest a need to diversify local economic activities).

Entrepreneurialism

In global fast-moving competitive markets, being at the forefront of products and processes has become ever more important for local economies. Local economic development strategies may emphasise innovation in processes and products, allowing local areas to capitalise on market potential. This can apply as much to services as to manufacturing: for example, producer service firms may become more competitive if they have up-to-date computer facilities or efficient information systems, with beneficial consequences for the satisfaction of customers. Local development practitioners may be able to measure the degree of innovation through indicators such as the rate of new firm formation or the number of patents for new products and processes.

To stimulate entrepreneurialism, local development practitioners can reflect upon the potential of strategies which encourage entrepreneurs to establish new businesses. This may include encouraging local universities to develop partnerships with local businesses and industries, or encouraging commercial activity amongst their researchers – to the benefit of both universities and the local economy. Relevant university activity may include spin-outs and enterprise creation, offering technical advice to local firms, developing courses for students that meet labour market needs, and the placement of students on industrial experience projects in local businesses. These kinds of knowledge-based approaches are increasingly popular in local economic development strategies, and can have important benefits in advancing or sustaining competitive advantage. There may also be an important challenge in encouraging more local procurement policies by public agencies and private businesses for their goods and services. These can generate greater local employment and help to ensure that more of the benefits of economic activity are retained in the local area.

Skill levels

There are often highly significant differences between areas in terms of levels of skills and these can impact directly on the locational choices of potential business investors making decisions about whether to site in one area as against another. This, in turn, can have major implications for the competitiveness of different local areas. Educational performance at school level often tends to "bunch" geographically, with some areas having high-performing schools and others with low performance as those parents who are economically able to determine their choice of housing move to areas with "good" schools, thereby creating a form of educational polarisation which can be reflected in variable levels of place competitiveness. Educational performance can have consequences for the desirability of some areas over others – and that too has economic impact because of the differential ability of areas to attract or retain skilled residents.

Equally, for many firms, the availability of high-quality graduate staff can be an important locational determinant. Places that lack universities, or good colleges, or that are not successful in retaining students in the area once they graduate, will therefore be at a disadvantage. By contrast, there are numerous instances around the world – the well-documented case of the Cambridges in the United Kingdom or Massachusetts in the United States for example – where local or regional economic competitiveness is in no small part a consequence of the presence of networks of globally significant research-based universities with links to local firms. The implication for local development strategies is either that policy objectives ought to help local areas to develop appropriate research bases through universities or other institutes, or that existing research capacity should be exploited more effectively for the benefit of the local and regional economy.

Premises

Local development policy makers may also reflect upon the availability of land and premises as a key determinant of the locational decisions of businesses. Large firms often require large attractive sites on which to locate, and increasingly many businesses look for "intelligent" buildings as an important aspect of their activities or high-profile buildings as a way of boosting their image. In a more general sense, both advanced manufacturing and service activities often look for attractive environments not merely to underline their self image, but also to attract high-quality staff. Here, the presence of good leisure and cultural facilities in an area can be important attractors. The supply of adequate sites and premises is limited in some urban areas, notably those in which degraded and fragmented stocks of brownfield land are a legacy of industrial restructuring or where high levels of economic activity create market pressures on available sites and premises.

Such considerations, not least in the context of urban areas, are clearly one of the justifications for the range of environmental and "cultural" interventions that may form one of the objectives of local development strategies. These, of course, are important aspects of local economic development in their own right, helping areas to benefit from demand for the consumption of leisure, retail or cultural services. But they are also important in a broader sense, in contributing to place attractiveness.

Desirable environments, iconic buildings and the creation of a "sense of place" can be significant in attracting new economic investment and facilitating local development.

Worklessness and ill health

The proportion of the working-age population that is in employment is one of the most significant elements of the gross value added (GVA) or gross domestic product (GDP) of an area. Whether formally defined unemployment is high or low, the overall proportion of economically active people in an area is a key aspect in the labour supply element of development. In some areas, large numbers of people who are not formally unemployed may remain outside the labour market for a variety of reasons: on the grounds of ill health or physical incapacity; through social constraints such as the need to look after children or infirm relatives; or sometimes simply through the discouragement that arises from the difficulty of finding jobs. These people represent potential unused "assets" that could raise the productivity of an area. For under-performing areas, local development strategies need to focus on both supply and demand sides in the labour market: helping to create new employment, but also cultivating a labour force with the appropriate skills, and removing barriers to entry to the workforce and increasing the supply of "employable" people. For high-performing local economies, too, development strategies can also focus on employability, trying to boost labour market participation rates in order to help meet the demand from employers.

In both cases, tackling health problems can represent an important element in the wider effort to increase the number of employable people, with consequent benefits for broader local competitiveness. Although many of the health problems of areas are constraints that can take a long time to correct, some can have more immediate impacts. For example, smoking-cessation projects or anti-drug programmes may result in alleviating common problems relatively quickly. Other approaches may focus on the provision of childcare and crèche facilities, or on appointing personal advisors who can help individuals to assess their suitability for certain jobs and assist in finding placements. In appraising potential objectives, local practitioners ought to consider these "softer" elements of economic development, which can be vital in creating the conditions in which competitiveness can flourish.

Communications

Accessibility can be an important element in determining the level of demand for the goods and services of local areas. Poor road and rail communications add to the cost of delivering products to market and, perhaps as importantly, can delay the response time and reliability of delivery. When, increasingly, just-in-time systems have become an important aspect of the supply of goods and services, the inability of an area to meet fluctuations in demand and to respond rapidly to changes in market demands can work to its disadvantage.

Considering the ways in which good electronic communications can make places more competitive could be an important focus of policy-maker deliberations in arriving at clear objectives. For example, not to be connected to broadband networks – or indeed not to have sufficient expertise to exploit the potential of electronic networks – can work to the disadvantage of local economies. Policy makers ought to reflect on the now extensive research evidence that some of the most successful regional and local economies around the world are those that are the most "wired up", with well-developed information and communication technology infrastructures supported by a workforce skilled in their maintenance and exploitation. For local development strategies, there is a need to consider how best to determine objectives that can encourage the upgrading of physical and electronic communications of areas in order to connect them better to the potential markets outside.

Travel to work

Labour markets operate over ever larger spatial areas as mobility increases and as the distance that people can commute grows ever longer. This represents an issue of growing importance in determining objectives for local development strategies. It means that local areas need to be well connected to employment nodes and that their residents may need to be prepared to travel further than in the past in order to access jobs that lie considerable distances away. This may in part be a question of improving public transport links, but may also be a matter of encouraging people to overcome any reluctance to consider working outside their immediate neighbourhood. For example, in many "traditional" industrial areas work was literally to be found on the doorstep since factories and houses were intermingled in a single neighbourhood and workers could walk short distances to work. Many such areas no longer have local jobs since factories have closed. Even where there are adequate transport links between the home and the workplace, there is sometimes a psychological barrier to be overcome in persuading local residents to look for work outside their neighbourhood rather than attempting to provide new jobs locally. Conversely, the challenge may be to persuade potential employers, who may "red-line" neighbourhoods that are thought to house unreliable or "difficult" residents, to offer jobs to people from such areas. Overcoming these kinds of obstacles can have important economic benefits, both for buoyant local areas (where the supply of labour can be improved and increased) and for lagging areas (where addressing labour market exclusion can have social as well as economic benefits).

A rather different but related situation may apply to areas with large proportions of ethnic minority households. Here there may be psychological barriers within the minority communities connected to the fear of real or perceived prejudice from people outside their local neighbourhoods. There may, in such circumstances, be a case for encouraging the establishment of ethnic-minority businesses or of re-training individuals from ethnic minorities to offer them specific skills that would enable them to seek jobs in the wider labour market.

Identifying priorities for local economic development strategies

In light of the many factors which contribute to local economic performance, we outline six issues that can usefully be explored by policy makers to help arrive at informed decisions with regard to the objectives of local development strategies.

Understanding local policy needs

While the overall objective to improve economic performance may be clear, the precise mix of relevant interventions may be much less clear, given the complex interactions between the socio-economic elements of the local context. This is a key issue for local development strategies, and one that merits especial attention in thinking about objectives.

It is therefore often helpful to develop models of inter-linkages between the numerous indicators of local conditions and to identify which elements pose especially difficult links in the "map" of inter-relationships. Disentangling cause and effect relationships in this respect is unrealistic, but an understanding of the complexity of the socio-economic context of the local areas in which development strategies are formulated is nevertheless vital if policy makers are to avoid developing initiatives which, while benefiting one aspect of an area's circumstances, fail to appreciate the knock-on consequences for other socio-economic dimensions. Diagrammatic representations of the interplay of socio-economic factors can provide one means by which policy makers can begin to develop an understanding of the potential impacts of local development strategies. Another approach is to try in a more qualitative way to "map" how an area might change in the future as a result of different forms of intervention.

Theory-based approaches, for example, have become increasingly popular as a means of appraising potential impacts arising from a programme's activities. Such approaches can encourage policy makers to develop scenarios dependent upon a range of possibilities in respect of a development strategy's impacts. The Logical Framework (LogFrame) method or "objectives-orientated project planning" provide approaches which emphasise the importance of identifying objectives and the anticipated impacts at different time points.

The LogFrame approach involves identifying the "programme logic" by exploring causal links in terms of a linear sequence, from inputs, via processes, to outputs, outcomes and final impact. Again, if used sensitively, this can be useful in taking account of the totality of the local socio-economic context and linking its change to quantitative measures of performance which relate to the different stages of a local development strategy. Where the more qualitative theory-based approaches can be of greater value, however, is in moving beyond simplistic causal links with which some variants of LogFrame are associated and taking account of multi-linear relationships. The point here is that policy makers seeking to develop objectives for local development strategies need to try to understand the dynamics of the process of neighbourhood change to consider how achievable the priorities are.

Linking the priorities of local development strategies

Questions about the geography of local development strategies raise the critical issue of how policy makers can devise approaches which marry the priorities of interventions at these different spatial scales. Evidence suggests that what happens at the regional or city scale in respect of development strategies is often divorced from intervention at the more localised neighbourhood level.

This frequent failure to develop complementary priorities at different spatial scales has often prompted central government efforts to promote more integrated and better co-ordinated policy making. "Joining-up" policy efforts – both horizontally across the different agencies involved in a particular development strategy in local areas, and vertically amongst the different tiers of government – is increasingly recognised as a priority for effective intervention. In determining the priorities for a local development strategy, this means considering three principal issues: first, identifying the relevant actors across public, private and voluntary sectors; second, ascertaining which of their activities could complement the potential foci of the strategy to be developed; and third, brokering agreement amongst the partners about the specific detail of the priorities and their respective roles in delivering them.

This, of course, is by no means a straightforward process. In many countries it has been compounded by the decline of monolithic government, the related fragmentation of institutions and the consequent proliferation of various agencies as part of wider governance networks. This has exacerbated the longer standing difficulties of agreeing objectives for local development strategies in a wider context of conflict between different functional departments of government, and between different levels of central and local government. Identifying and agreeing shared priorities represents a considerable challenge where deeply embedded institutional agendas prevail, and where cultures of inter-agency working are poorly developed. The result, in some instances, is that exhortations for joining up never result in effective partnership working, and any collaborative activity tends to be restricted to high-level discussion centring on uncontroversial issues about which there is a high degree of pre-existing consensus. In contrast, the detailed practical issues – synchronising funding cycles, integrating monitoring and evaluation approaches, sacrificing narrow, institution-specific goals – are more likely to be ignored, in case their contentiousness threatens the stability of inter-institutional coalitions.

These are issues to which national governments have become increasingly attuned. Attention has been devoted to devising incentives for collaborative working, moving beyond mere exhortation. One particular priority has been to try to ensure that mainstream public expenditure – on routine production and consumption services – dovetails with the objectives of local development strategies. The longer term aspirations of such approaches are that the outcomes of time-limited, area-based interventions should last beyond the end of a policy, programme or strategy, and that future mainstream expenditure should routinely and automatically perform the tasks previously tackled through special, short-term and spatially focused initiatives. In these ways, policy makers can embed within their interventions a more long-term approach that has often been lacking in many local development strategies. The principal difficulty, however, is that attention to the specifics of mainstreaming is often not uppermost in policy makers' minds when determining priorities. If local development strategies are to have impacts that last, thinking about how best to prioritise objectives which relate to the integration of local development strategies and mainstream spend is vital.

Identifying and including agents of change

It is important not just to think of established state and quasi-state agencies, but also to involve actors from other stakeholder groups. This can mean business groupings, where the challenge is to engage firms which tend not to look outward or which lack well-developed traditions of corporate social responsibility, but which nevertheless exert substantial influence both on local labour markets and, through the multiplier effects of their activities, on the wider economies of the areas in which they are located. It can also mean involving local residents, where again the challenge is partly one of involving those most marginalised from existing decision-making processes. While involving established groups such as resident or tenant associations, amenity groups, business, commerce and trade alliances, voluntary sector bodies or trade unions is often a practicable short-term goal, it is not necessarily the case that people drawn from these groupings will be representative, especially if the objective of a local development strategy is to involve marginalised or excluded residents in a meaningful way.

Whether for businesses or residents, engaging the "hardest to reach" groups, as well as those displaying a readiness at the outset to become involved, can play a vital role in contributing to a local strategy's effectiveness. And while governments may urge local agencies to involve an inclusive range of participants in the policy-making and delivery process, this is often difficult to reconcile with the parallel stress on performance management and the output-oriented mentality it inculcates amongst local actors.

In all these respects, a key issue for local development strategies is how to develop objectives that can help to build effective local capacity. This applies in particular to certain types of areas: for example, to rural areas, where the scattered nature of people and firms can constrain the extent to which (or the pace at which) capacity develops; or in marginalised urban areas, characterised by poorly developed social capital and a reluctance to get involved in decision-making processes linked to local economic development. In both instances, practitioners ought to look towards some of the best practice examples of efforts to build capacity and involve different stakeholder groups. In rural areas, for example, the European Union LEADER II and LEADER+ initiatives have actively encouraged community "animation" and capacity building (for example, through community-based local action groups established in Ireland's development areas).

Ensuring durability of outcome

One of the problems that frequently arises from the absence of joined-up ownership and implementation of local development strategies is that any gains are more likely to be ephemeral than if a range of partners can show continued support over a long period. Locally based development strategies have often been viewed as fundamentally short term in nature. In part, this is a conscious and explicit approach, where limited-life intervention can be justified as a means of restoring market equilibrium or because they are experimental in nature. More commonly, however, it is the result of the politically expedient nature of locally focused intervention – which provides a demonstrable illustration of political interest in resolving problems, often generating tangible, physical results.

Whatever the precise explanation, it is clear that too often long-term strategy is not given due priority in developing local development plans. The implication is that alertness to the timeframe around which local intervention is to occur must be an important priority for policy makers in devising objectives. To do so is difficult, however, in the context of pressure to demonstrate impact over the short term, not least to satisfy demands imposed by internal and external audits of performance and policy efficiency. This, in turn, reinforces the need for local development to be integrated with mainstream services, which tend typically to be viewed as permanent aspects of local governance – in contrast to the perception of local development initiatives as fleeting "stopgaps". Changing such perceptions has therefore to be a key priority if objectives are to be defined satisfactorily and policy efficacy to be maximised. Prior assessment, as part of the evaluation process, clearly has to take account of the extent to which long-term involvement of partners, and a realism about the gestation time of the impacts of any strategy, are embedded in local development objectives.

Identifying target groups and ensuring the distribution of benefit

The question of "who benefits" from policy intervention has, of course, long preoccupied policy makers. In crude terms, local development strategies have, at various times, been viewed either as overly concerned with particular groups, whether businesses, sectoral client groups or geographically defined residents. This, in turn, has generated criticism of the mal-distribution of benefit arising from a local development strategy. Local policy makers ought at the outset to be clear about who are the intended beneficiaries of a policy, and to spell out in detail the mechanism for ensuring that impacts are distributed along the lines envisaged. Too often this has proved not be the case: the archetypical instance is the property-led approach to local economic development, where state-led investment to improve malfunctioning local land and property markets is assumed to benefit not just land owners, developers and occupiers of sites and premises, but the wider array of residents in and around the intervention area, through the nebulous process of "trickle down".

While such approaches are now widely discredited, they do provide a reminder of the need not only to identify the desired beneficiaries of intervention, but also the need for policy makers to develop the means by which local markets can be managed to ensure that the intended recipients benefit. This means reflecting on the ways in which objectives can relate in clear ways to particular target groups or areas. It also means thinking about how best to tailor intervention so that impacts "stick" to the right area and group. For example, any locally based development strategy has to be conscious from the beginning that benefits within an intervention area could "leak" outwards to surrounding areas. Equally, there needs to be an awareness that benefit can be displaced from surrounding areas, in which case a zero-sum game results (even if there are distributional arguments in favour of shuffling development from one area to another). The issue here is that these problems can only be averted if policy makers are aware of them when formulating local strategies at the outset.

Ensuring that monitoring and evaluation continuously inform the updating of objectives

Identifying clear objectives with regard to monitoring and evaluation must also be a key priority for policy makers in any prior assessment or *ex ante* appraisal of potential objectives for a local development strategy. This means thinking not only about the basic requirements of funders and/or auditors of performance, but also about the ways in which monitoring and evaluation objectives can be used to contribute to the development and refinement of local development strategies. To do this, there is a need to avoid purely audit-influenced monitoring and evaluation arrangements which are seen as bureaucratic and burdensome by local policy actors, but rather those that have a demonstrably useful role in helping to promote "organisational learning" and the improvement of policy.

Governments are becoming more sensitised to these issues in developing guidelines for monitoring and evaluation. In the United Kingdom, revised guidance on the evaluation of regeneration programmes reflects a shift away from simply enumerating project outputs in relation to public money expended, and instead emphasises the importance of defining outcome-based measures of performance which relate directly to policy objectives (ODPM, 2003). The guidance cautions against over-reliance on readily quantifiable outcome measures. While "value-for-money" considerations continue to be important, these guidelines also recognise the need to relate monitoring and evaluation to the evolution of policy itself, encouraging formative approaches which can help to refine objectives during the course of a local development strategy.

Defining Objectives – Summary of Do's and Don'ts

Do's

- Consider which statistical indicators ought to be assembled as part of the appraisal process, and which benchmark areas should be selected to help in identifying local development strategy objectives.
- Consider the scale at which intervention should occur and ensure that objectives complement strategies directed towards different scales.
- Identify and include agents of change, building capacity for stakeholder involvement where it is lacking.
- Ensure that development strategy objectives are written with the long-term durability of outcomes in mind, and with the emphasis on a long-term perspective.
- Develop an understanding of the local economic and social context and its implications for the performance of the local economy.
- Identify the target groups to benefit from a local development strategy and ensure that objectives are constructed so that outcomes are distributed equitably.
- Develop at the outset clear objectives for future monitoring and evaluation of policy.

Don'ts

- Don't assemble data at too aggregated a scale, limiting the degree to which it can be used flexibly. Assemble data only for a particular time period, preventing an appreciation of the trajectory of local economic performance over time.
- Don't ignore the relationship between the target area for a local development strategy, and the surrounding area – an appreciation of the effects of intervention of one upon the other is essential.
- Don't exclude particular stakeholder groups from the process of building a consensus about which objectives to pursue as part of a local development strategy.
- Don't focus purely on objectives which relate to short-term outcomes, but which ignore their longer term sustainability in the absence of continued intervention.
- Don't adopt a one-size-fits-all development strategy which ignores the specificities of the local area.
- Don't rely purely on market forces to distribute benefits, particularly to those groups most marginalised from local labour markets.
- Don't assume that monitoring and evaluation arrangements can be established after a development strategy has begun to be implemented. Monitoring and evaluation should not be viewed as burdensome, but should feed directly into the refinement of policy, as a development strategy evolves.

References

ODPM (2003), "Assessing the Impacts of Spatial Interventions, Regeneration, Renewal and Regional Development Main Guidance", Interdepartmental Group on the EGRUP Review, Office of the Deputy Prime Minister, London.

Chapter 2
Identifying the Options for Intervention

by
Paul Lawless

The process of defining alternative options and selecting a preferred choice is a critical element in the overall process of strategy development. However it has not traditionally received a great deal of attention, because of factors such as partners being reluctant to subject tried and trusted approaches to more objective assessment.

A number of key principles should be adopted to help identify options. The process of identifying options should be as transparent as possible and it should involve reflecting backwards to defined objectives and forwards to anticipated impacts. It is also important to accept that doing nothing may be the best solution – at least in the short run.

In building up options, partners need to reflect on a range of criteria including the areas of intervention being addressed; the balance between harder physical investment projects as opposed to softer skills associated with enhanced competitiveness; assumed beneficiaries, geographical scale, time horizons, any financial and legal considerations; actors and agencies needed for the effective implementation of options; appropriate management and strategic steer and sustainability.

In selecting the preferred option, partners will need to consider the degree to which options achieve defined objectives and the full costs and benefits of risks associated with different options.

The impact and outcomes of different options is briefly considered here but discussed at length in the next chapter.

Introduction

Identifying possible options and subsequently selecting a "best fit" solution is a key process in making good local development strategies. Yet despite its importance it is probably true to say that it has received **less attention** than many other steps in the strategy development process. This is because of a number of **obstacles**, including:

- There can be a tendency to go along with the "conventional or accepted view" of what makes a good strategy; stakeholders may believe that there is an "obvious" way of doing things.
- Devising options can be seen as difficult and time consuming.
- Partners may be unhappy about long-standing favoured projects being subject to what they can see as irrelevant appraisal.
- Actors may be simply unaware of the importance of identifying options for appraisal.
- There may be a lack of specialist skills in this area, which can prove to be a particular problem for smaller organisations.

As a result of the impact of these kinds of factors the **evidence base for devising options and selecting a preferred option is thin**. Nevertheless identifying and appraising options is a **critical element** in the process of strategy development. In particular it should:

- Provide an ideal opportunity to think of new ways of doing things and of avoiding past errors.
- Ensure that different options are subject to fair and rigorous assessment.
- Help achieve value for money.
- Ensure all key partners have a voice in driving forward the preferred strategy.
- Bring new thinking to the table.

This chapter explores options for intervention within **four sub-themes**:

1. Key principles underpinning the identification of options.
2. Criteria to be employed in building up options.
3. Bringing together key criteria through three practical examples.
4. Identifying the preferred option.

Identifying options: some key principles

In identifying options and selecting a preferred strategy, it may be useful to bear in mind a number of **key principles** which should help partners develop a robust approach. Four are outlined below:

It's part of a bigger process

Identifying options is only one element in making good strategies; it is important therefore both to:

- **Reflect backwards** to ensure that defined options can meet the overall objectives of the development strategy, a process discussed in the previous chapter. In many circumstances the more precise the objectives, the easier it will be to select options and to identify a preferred strategy. Vague overarching objectives are often of little value in assessing options.
- It is also important to **look forwards** to make sure that the preferred option has a plausible chance of meeting anticipated impacts, an issue which is considered in detail in the next chapter.

Defining options thus plays a role in linking together different components in the strategy making process. In particular it bridges two key components in the overall process: "defining objectives" and "assessing impacts".

Proportionality

Identifying options is clearly a centrally important element in strategy development. However it is important that partners adopt an approach which is proportionate to the strategy concerned. More substantial local development strategies impacting wide areas and longer time periods, usually involving a range of sectors, will generally justify considerable investment in defining and assessing options; smaller proposals will merit less effort.

Transparency

Subject to any commercial confidentialities, the processes by which options are identified and a preferred choice selected should be as transparent as possible. This helps to create trust across partners, maximises contributions from different actors, and ensures that a full range of options is addressed. Whilst transparency may seem an obvious principle to adopt, there can be circumstances where some partners prefer to contain the process in order to reduce the range of options and hence to improve the chances of their "own approach" being adopted; such pressures should be resisted.

It may be best to do nothing, at least for now

Partners will generally assume that economic and employment problems necessitate development strategies. In most circumstances this will be a perfectly reasonable assumption to make. But there may be instances where doing nothing makes sense, at least in the short to medium term. For instance new transport infrastructure may be about to come on stream in the near future or recently launched national policy initiatives will have implications for proposed local development strategies. There could also be cases where partners may wish to see how previous interventions pan out before committing to new strategies or reconfirming support for existing initiatives. Doing nothing is unlikely to appeal to many partners, but it may have merits in the shorter run; at the very least benefits arising from identified options should be compared with a "doing nothing" scenario.

Building up the options: key criteria

Identifying options for local development strategies will normally involve the consideration of a number of criteria, nine of which are considered below. Options for local development strategies will rarely need to refer to all of these. But those charged with creating options for appraisal may find this a useful checklist:

- Areas of intervention.
- Harder edges or softer skills?
- Beneficiaries.
- Geographical scale.
- Timing.
- Financial and legal considerations.
- Actors.
- Management and governance.
- Sustainability.

Areas of intervention

Local strategies will vary in the degree to which they focus on different **sectors of the economy**. In some instances partners will be seeking to intensify, or diversify away from, agriculture. There may also be opportunities for enhancing some manufacturing activities. However, increasingly there is likely to be more of an emphasis on increasing economic activity and employment in various service sectors. Sometimes this may involve looking to build on relatively low-value service sector employment and activity such as retailing, warehousing or call-centre employment. In other instances partners may wish to emphasise education and training, and in others provide a framework within which innovative business services can thrive. In practice many local development strategies will of course be seeking to enhance activity across a range of sectors.

Harder edges or softer skills?

Actors need to ensure they achieve an appropriate balance between harder edged physical investments on the one hand, with strategies designed to boost skills, innovation and social capital, on the other. Particularly in relation to regional or sub-regional development, there has been an inclination in some quarters to support harder edged developments: roads, infrastructural projects, new commercial or tourism development projects, and so on. Increasingly, however, the emphasis has shifted towards enhancing economic competitiveness across regions and cities. In order to do this agencies will need to understand the importance of a different set of interventions designed to build innovation, create robust and mutually supportive business institutions, and boost social capital In practice, of course, many development strategies will of necessity look to both supporting physical investment, whilst at the same time driving forward "softer" skills.

Beneficiaries

Some local development strategies may be targeted at specific socio-demographic groups. Instances where this might occur include:

- Integrated training, basic education and job search initiatives for residents in deprived localities.
- Language courses, job training initiatives and job search programmes for immigrant populations.
- Schemes to enhance skills and job awareness amongst young people.
- Programmes specifically designed to boost female employment on specific sectors such as engineering.
- Job search projects for older male workers made redundant from contracting industrial sectors or from agriculture.

Developing options will often require partners to be explicit about whether particular groups are to be targeted and how.

Geographical scale

In developing options for appraisal, partners will need to make clear the geographical boundaries within which interventions are to occur. These can vary considerably:

- Some initiatives, such as training projects, may be designed to cover entire cities or regions.
- Other projects, such as schemes to provide personalised job mentoring, may be directed at those living in specific neighbourhoods.
- And some initiatives may focus on more narrowly circumscribed localities: the physical redevelopment of a redundant industrial site in order to create an integrated business park and educational facility, for instance.

Defining geographical scale is important in informing the development of options. It allows partners to appreciate the scale of activity; it helps focus intervention on specific areas; and it clarifies which partners are to adopt which particular remits within which defined intervention areas.

Timing

Time horizons are important in developing options for appraisal. Some proposed interventions, such as training or business support schemes, can be devised and implemented over relatively short time horizons. Others, such as major redevelopment proposals, will take longer to devise and implement.

Partners need to be clear about the time horizons involved, not least because these will have implications for the phasing of demands on agency resources. In this context it makes sense to see the time equation impacting in two rather different circumstances:

- One where similar development proposals are being considered.
- As opposed to circumstances where different approaches are being proposed to meet longer term objectives.

Here is one example to illustrate the former. A new training programme is required to meet the labour demands of a major inward investment project involving some research and development and production of a new generation of flat screen TVs. Partners are faced with several options:

- A substantial "front-loaded" programme designed rapidly to boost local skills across the board.
- An initial universal "first base" training programme followed up by more specialist inputs for some.
- Developing longer term training modules in local schools and adult education colleges.

Timing becomes important here in at least two ways: ensuring that training packages meet the immediate labour demands arising from inward investment projects; and also making certain that the funding packages for different training schemes complement the availability of resources from development agencies.

There can however be circumstances when ultimate objectives can be met through markedly different options. To give one example: a major port is implementing new dock facilities specifically designed to allow easier access for larger ships. This will lead to the closure of an established port area close to the city centre. The ultimate outcome is to revitalise this redundant area for new economic activity. Partners are hence faced with real choices. The area could potentially be developed as a new "e-business" project; an educational and training hub; a centre for arts and cultural activities; a major retail park; new business units; or a mixture of some or all of these activities.

In this context, time represents one of the key criteria by which different options will be assessed:

- Some schemes could be implemented more rapidly than others. Partners may find developers happy to build, say, standard business units as quickly as possible, but would the interests of the city and its region ultimately be better served by looking to develop an "e-business" or cultural facility which will take more time to implement, but which might be more sustainable in the longer run?
- Partners may be reluctant to look too far ahead because of uncertainty about the continuing availability of some funding streams. They may consider it better to implement less than perfect proposals immediately, rather than face the danger of funding sources being reduced or eliminated.
- And it can be also be difficult to delay too long if proposals require political approval in some form or other; understandably politicians are generally reluctant to appear indecisive.

There is a further issue within the overall dimension of timing. There can be circumstances where it is important to make a distinction between the time required to carry out interventions, as opposed to the time horizons involved in the realisation of impacts. To give one example, a largely rural region has seen further rationalisation of land ownership, enhanced mechanisation, and associated reductions in agricultural employment. Programmes are put in place to enhance entrepreneurial skills, help new "non-rural" firms, boost rural tourism, retrain ex-rural workers, and so on. These interventions can be implemented relatively quickly. But outcomes in the way of, say, moving ex-agricultural workers into new sectors, reversing population loss, instilling entrepreneurial attitudes, building social capital, creating non-rural jobs, and so on, may take many years to feed through. If partners identify options designed to achieve deep-seated change, they need to accept that whatever interventions are adopted, outcome change can take many years to occur.

Financial and legal considerations

In some instances the financial and legal implications of options will need to be considered. A number of questions surrounding **financing** are likely to emerge in developing options for appraisal. In particular there will be a need to carefully:

- Estimate the full costs of options.
- Identify which costs fall on which partners and when for each option.
- Highlight any financial contingencies: for instance it may be that some sources of funding can only be employed if "matched" funding has been secured from elsewhere.

In some instances options will also need to address legal implications and impediments. These will vary depending on the prevailing legal system, the scale of the local development strategy being considered, patterns of land ownership, and so on. But issues which may crop up include:

- Establishing land ownership, which can constrain the timing and nature of development, especially in older, mixed use, industrial areas where identifying ultimate land ownership can be costly and time consuming.
- It may become obvious that the implementation of some options requires land acquisition; this can be achieved through normal market processes. More often it will ultimately require some form of compulsory acquisition which can prove expensive in terms of resources and time.

- As is discussed immediately below, many strategies require active support from a wide range of key actors and agencies. In many cases co-operation across agencies can be achieved on a purely informal basis. In some instances however there may be a need to create some form of legal entity through which to implement larger projects. Although this process will take time and will have financial implications, it may be necessary in order to provide a clear indication of the timing and scale of financial and other commitments falling on partners.

Actors and agencies

Implementing local development strategies will require the involvement and support of different **actors and agencies**. Agencies provide the overall framework within which local development strategies are implemented. But the influence of key individuals should not be underestimated. In some circumstances one key actor having senior responsibility in a development agency can play a quite decisive role in devising options and selecting a preferred strategy.

Naturally the impact of actors and agencies will vary considerably across different regions and countries. It will generally be the case too that the more complex the proposal, the more actors and agencies will need to be involved. In theory those involved may include:

- **Local government**, which will often prove to be a key agency. Typically local governments know more about the issues surrounding particular problems; they will often have access to, or influence over, financial and legal resources; they are democratically elected and thus represent a source of political legitimacy and accountability; and they can help push developments along if delays are encountered. In many circumstances local government will be the key facilitator in driving forward the process of defining options and identifying an agreed approach.
- **Regional and national government**, which can also play a critical role in pushing forward larger development strategies. In some countries regional tiers of administration play little, if any, role in development; in others they have an important function in funding and facilitating development. In virtually all states national governments have some influence over the legal and financial frameworks within which local schemes are implemented. Options will need to be embedded within the wider institutional context: there is no point in proposing possibilities when it is known they will run into barriers set by regional and/or national governments.

- **Local business**, whose role will vary across both countries and strategies. But the private sector can play the key role in helping to fund projects where commercial returns are possible; in providing expertise in relation to markets, business needs, prospects, and risks; and in easing constraints on development. In some more disadvantaged localities or areas where traditional industry or agricultural output has declined, the local business sector may be limited in size and scope. But options for development need to set out the degree to which proposals are based upon the needs of, and the extent to which they will in turn support, local business. In many instances one effective way of getting the views and involvement of business will be through direct contact with chambers of commerce or their equivalents.

- **Local communities** can have an important function in helping to devise options. In some instances local communities, or perhaps key players within the locality, may have strong evidence-based views on the desirability and impact of different options. Across the developed world some of the most iconic urban developments have emerged from the strongly held views of local community groups.

- **Voluntary and "third arm" organisations** can be important in helping to drive forward local development. Some cities and regions have thriving "informal sectors". They may be important in helping to devise and select options. For instance they may have access to particular funding streams not available to other organisations. There may too be instances where projects such as, say, training schemes or initiatives designed to boost small businesses would have a different cost basis if implemented by the "informal sector" than would be the case if run by the private sector. There may too be implications for the sustainability of strategies if these are implemented by informal sector organisations. The latter tend to have a long term commitment to an area or client group and often plan to re-invest any surpluses into ensuring the sustainability of the scheme involved. These objectives may be rather different to those assumed by the private sector or indeed local government.

- In some countries **social partners**, notably trade unions, have a role to play in devising options. Social partners can have important insights into options for local development. These might especially revolve around the need for labour market interventions including the desirability of new training or job mentoring schemes, for instance.

- Finally **delivery agencies** should almost always be regarded as key actors in devising options. Circumstances will vary across states. In some countries local government is likely to have a key role in implementing changes across a wide range of agendas including economic development, education, training, transport, land development, and so on. But in many countries there has been a trend for local government to lose some functions to dedicated delivery agencies with a specific remit for, say, labour market training, land acquisition and development, public transport, and so on. Furthermore in many countries planning and development powers for specific, often rundown, localities may well have been vested in dedicated development agencies. Options need to be embedded in the plans and funding streams of these organisations.

In many circumstances local development strategies will not require a substantial input from the full range of actors and agencies outlined above. But in devising options it is important to ensure that those key to implementation are involved from the outset in helping to define possibilities, and in selecting a preferred solution.

Because of this potential range of organisations involved it may often be the case that local development strategies require the creation of a formal or informal **partnership** across different agencies. This can have implications for devising options. To give one example, a local development strategy is needed to increase formation and survival rates of new companies emerging from more disadvantaged groups and localities. This could be implemented in at least two ways:

- By building on an existing local business development agency funded by central government which has a well-established programme, but which does not provide much longer term "hand-holding" support to new firms.
- Through a more time-consuming route based on a partnership across a range of local agencies including local government, community groups, local businesses and third arm bodies in order to implement a strategy to create and support new firms emerging from disadvantaged groups in the local labour market.

These strategies present different options for addressing a particular need. The first may require relatively little in the way of partnership work. The latter will entail time and effort in building up and sustaining a partnership across a range of agencies. But in the longer run the second option may be more likely to achieve defined objectives.

However, although partnership working may often appear a sensible way forward, this type of working **can impose "costs"**:

- It will take time to establish and run an effective partnership.

- Some agencies can see partnership working as lacking focus and direction.
- Agencies will need to be convinced that resources they might be putting into partnership working represents value for money.
- There can be particular problems in maintaining a collaborative approach when partnerships include agencies with very different skills, capacities and attitudes.

Ultimately some larger planned developments may well require a partnership of some kind. In other instances it may be that a lead agency is best placed to devise options and drive forward a resultant strategy, consulting where necessary with other relevant bodies. Partnership working is not a "cost-free" approach.

Management and governance

Local development strategies will need day-to-day management, but often also a strategic steer. Considerations which need to be taken into account in devising options here might include:

- **The quality of management**: in devising options it may be necessary to consider the experience, expertise and leadership qualities of managers in driving forward agreed local development strategies, as well as their technical competencies in areas such as resource planning, human resources and information technology.
- **Strategic steer**: depending on the nature of the strategy, it may be that options need to consider the issue of strategic direction; this could become especially significant where a range of agencies is involved. In such circumstances it may be important to establish some kind of "Project Board" to regularly review progress and to address constraints undermining progress.
- **Monitoring and evaluation**: larger projects in particular should provide a clear indication that they have thought through financial and output monitoring, how evaluation might best be undertaken, and mechanisms by which changes can be introduced if monitoring and evaluation point to problems in implementation.

Sustainability

An increasing emphasis will need to be placed on all aspects of sustainability. In many instances the development of options and the selection of a preferred approach will need to consider the impact of proposals on:

- The local ecology.
- The totality of environmental change arising through land use, transport and energy implications of different options.
- The degree to which strategies can be sustained through time.
- The implications of proposals on all sectors in society.
- And hence an assessment of the full environmental consequences arising from each proposed option.

Pulling it all together: some examples

The criteria explored above provide an indication of factors to be taken into account in developing options for local development strategies. In practice these criteria will need to be pulled together to create a series of potential options from which one is ultimately selected. Practical examples are one way of illustrating how the process might operate. Four examples are outlined below:

1. Strategies to enhance local skills.
2. Strategies to boost local entrepreneurship and innovation.
3. Options for evolving rural regions.
4. Options involved in redeveloping outmoded urban economies.

Case Study 1. Upgrading the local skill base: boosting local economic development

The problem

There are often substantial pockets of unskilled people in many developed cities and rural regions. Some may be economically inactive, others working in sectors requiring few skills. Yet at the same time there can be regional skills shortages in other sectors. There is often therefore a need to provide suitable training for unskilled groups which can both assist in their own personal and economic development, whilst at the same time help to ease local labour market bottlenecks. Government wishes to establish a sustainable training strategy for unskilled people, with a particular emphasis on supporting pockets of new immigrants from less developed countries.

Several options are possible

Do nothing. If labour shortages become acute, firms may in the end enhance their own training programmes. But experience suggests firms may be more inclined to poach trained labour, thus creating inflationary pressures in the labour market.

Use one supplier to provide a standardised training programme. In many developed countries there will be a private sector infrastructure through which "standard" training programmes can be carried out. Those charged with the local development strategy know these courses can be put on relatively easily and they appear to have a successful track record. But there are concerns that private trainers may simply "cream off" those easiest to train, will not really attack the issue of new immigrant communities, and once targets have been achieved, will simply move on.

Pull together key delivery agencies. One option would be to pull together all existing development, educational and training agencies in the region. In many countries there can be a relatively sophisticated network of agencies with some role to play in training. There are advantages to this "agency partnership" approach in that it uses existing networks of agencies which are going to be around for the longer haul. On the other hand relationships between agencies may not always run smoothly; this approach will require careful partnership working; and not all agencies will have strong records of successful engagement with more deprived communities.

Use social enterprise. A more radical solution would be to create or build on local social enterprises. In some countries this may not be an option. But in others there will be an existing or potential network of social enterprises or voluntary sector bodies through which training programmes might be implemented. Such an approach may be seen as riskier than some other options, and there may be concerns about the management and regular delivery of the programme. But there could be real advantages too. Social enterprises and voluntary groups tend to have more of a local presence in deprived localities. They often have a history of working with immigrant communities. They will also be more inclined to address the problems of the most unskilled. They will not be driven solely by throughput targets. And they will stay around to help build up social capital.

Case Study 2. Entrepreneurship and local innovation

The problem

Many older industrialised cities and regions are seeking to enhance entrepreneurship and innovation. As traditional manufacturing employment and economic activity contracts, regions can find themselves lacking firms likely to create new jobs and boost economic activity in innovative sectors.

Options

Do nothing. This would not generally be an option here. Market forces are of themselves unlikely to resolve this problem for many older industrial regions.

Upgrade the existing economic base. One option would be to try and upgrade the existing economic base by using innovation and development agencies, loans, grants, beacon schemes, learning projects and so on to encourage existing firms to become more entrepreneurial and innovative. This would have the advantage of building on existing firms and sectors and it may help these companies to survive within their existing markets. But as an approach it is unlikely to enhance innovation in new or more advanced sectors, and may well lead to a further reduction in employment.

Create business incubators. One micro-approach would be to bring together local government, development agencies and the private sector in order to create a series of business incubators solely housing firms in pre-defined innovative sectors. Innovation would be encouraged through technical and financial training and support, assistance in marketing, mentoring of smaller firms by larger ones, mutual help across firms, and so on. But the evidence base suggests that many enterprises which start off in incubators do not always thrive or even survive; hence this option might best be seen as only part of a long-term programme of change.

Support innovation clusters. Clusters have attracted considerable interest in many developed countries and regions. Typically governments and development agencies, working with the private sector, attempt to support firms within specific pre-defined innovative sectors such as biomedicine, pharmaceuticals, and electronics. Support here may include providing land and infrastructure; a high-quality architectural and physical environment; creating an agency through which to develop, finance and market the defined sector, etc. Such an approach has the merits of focus and creating clear market messages. But those considering this option should also be aware that the evidence is very mixed regarding the value of clusters, other than those located in specially favoured localities such as Cambridge in the United Kingdom.

Encourage inward investment. Finally there is the option of seeking to enhance the entrepreneurial base through the inward investment of new projects. Deprived cities and regions may be in a strong position here in that partners are often in a position to offer attractive packages based on immediately available serviced land, infrastructural investment, local university "know-how", relatively cheap labour, and a regime of grants and loans available to incoming firms. On the other hand, competition for inward investments in innovative sectors is fierce, not simply within, but also across, countries. In addition such investments may not be sustainable in the longer run: the more distant a production facility is from company headquarters, the more likely it is to be closed in times of economic retrenchment. And the evidence is by no means conclusive that having a new major production facility will create positive spill-over effects in the region concerned in the way of encouraging innovative small and medium-sized enterprises (SMEs).

Case Study 3. Options for evolving rural regions

The problem

Rural regions in developed countries have been subject to considerable change: rationalisation of land ownership, further mechanisation, ecological problems, changes in subsidy regimes, new health and safety regulations undermining local markets, declining agricultural employment, depopulation, and so on. A common underlying imperative is the need for economic diversification.

Options

Do nothing. This is unlikely to address the inter-related set of problems impacting on many rural regions.

Downstream agricultural diversification. There may be some opportunities to support spin-offs from mainstream agricultural productions: further processing of agricultural products, enhanced output of organic produce, and so on. But this is unlikely to make many inroads into rural unemployment. Some activities such as organic produce may also be dependent on a range of specialist requirements: production skills, an ability to operate in niche markets, and favourable prevailing regulations.

Stimulate local demand. One approach would be to push forward diversification through "bottom-up" demand from farmers, entrepreneurs, local authorities, and so on. Typically demand is likely to revolve around small-scale tourist projects, conversion of farm buildings into small workshops, leisure activities, and so on. Demand for training or infrastructural support would be met by local agencies on an *ad hoc* basis. This incremental approach may be a realistic option in many circumstances. But it not going to change things radically.

Opt for an integrated approach. Agencies may decide that the scale of rural change and depopulation requires a more integrated approach. Typically this might revolve around a partnership of agencies devising a development strategy based on dedicated projects in one or two pre-defined regional "hubs". Development agencies and business would agree to focus investment in these defined localities. Such investment might include new retail complexes, housing projects, new markets, business centres, entrepreneurship training, business support, and so on. Defining such centres may be the most plausible way of dealing with decline across regions. But there will be opposition from "non-selected" towns and regions. And of itself, it may not lead to regional transformation.

Consider iconic development. There may be an opportunity to be more radical in some regions. Policies designed to focus growth in one or two regional centres might be complemented by one major national or even international development. This option may not be available for all regions. But there will be possibilities for some. These are generally likely to be based on leisure, tourism, gambling and "sustainable development" projects. It seems highly likely for instance that there will be continuing demand for major leisure complexes offering a range of pursuits for different social groups. There may be other possibilities, too. If national and regional governments can agree, a new rural university, for instance, can have all kinds of educational, reputational and entrepreneurial benefits.

Case Study 4. Reinvigorating depressed urban economies

The problem

One issue affecting many urban economies is what to do with specific localities subject to severe economic retrenchment. Even in successful cities there will often be rundown areas where integrated local development strategies are needed. It may be that a port area has closed, or a major industrial zone declined, or older commercial and retail developments lost their economic rationale. A number of possible options are likely to emerge.

Options

Do nothing. Market investment is unlikely to occur unless some infrastructural and human capital investment is undertaken.

Acquire land and install infrastructure. One relatively minimalist approach might be for government and development agencies to acquire and develop disused or underused land, and install appropriate physical infrastructure. This should provide a development framework for private investment. Such an approach will probably receive general support. In addition it will help ensure that limited public sector resources are used to lever in private investment. There can be technical problems however, including identifying prevailing land ownership. Leaving the market to invest is likely to also lead to a somewhat *ad hoc* mix of land uses and activities. A more focussed approach might lead to longer term economic benefits for the city/region concerned.

Opt for an integrated approach. Government, development agencies, the private sector and voluntary groups may decide to implement a holistic strategy managed by a partnership of key players. Such an approach might focus on physical developments, associated training and educational programmes, support for innovative SMEs, etc. This option would give players a better handle on guiding longer term strategic development. But it may be hard to sustain a successful partnership through time. For instance government may wish to take a longer term view, whereas the market will want to see developments occurring more quickly. There are often also tensions between, on the one hand, governments and development agencies looking to support new, advanced sectors, and, on the other hand, local businesses and local communities wishing to renew existing economic activity.

Consider "smallholding". In some circumstances, especially in very depressed localities, there may be a case for "opening up" parts of larger development sites for new economic activity. Subject to health and safety regulations, in principle any use would be allowed. This may be seen as an effective way of encouraging entrepreneurship and in focussing environmentally unappealing activities in one locality. However, in most circumstances partners will be looking to improve environmental standards as an instrument through which to create sustainable development for the benefit of all groups in society.

Support mega developments. In many cities, especially those subject to considerable economic restructuring, there will be pressure to use developable sites for mega projects such as convention centres, new stadia, casinos, major leisure facilities, large retail projects, and so on. Benefits can flow from such options: development is likely to occur quickly; these schemes can have an iconic status; and they will provide unskilled jobs for local people. But there can be a downside, too. These kinds of projects are land hungry, making more integrated, balanced approaches difficult to implement. They will compete with similar facilities in other cities. They may not be sustainable. They tend to offer limited opportunities through which to enhance innovation in the wider region. And generally they offer relatively little in the way of more highly skilled and paid jobs.

Consider the eco-park. Finally some cities will increasingly look to "the sustainable market" as a rationale for new developments. Projects embedded within such strategies might include sustainable energy schemes, eco-tourist activities, sustainable sports and leisure activities, incubators through which to support new enterprises in sustainable sectors, and so on. Such options may well be entirely appropriate and reflect emerging markets. But there is not a strong evidence base against which to test such ideas and some partners may regard this kind of option as having unproven longer term benefits.

Identifying the preferred option

Finally it is important here to consider some of the issues involved in selecting a preferred option. The next chapter addresses mechanisms through which to identify impacts and outcomes arising from different options. In many instances those assessing options will use evidence in relation to expected impact as the most important criterion by which to select a preferred strategy.

But option selection will often need to encompass other considerations. This may be especially true where larger scale proposals are being considered. In these instances, in addition to each option being subject to an impact assessment, partners may also wish to reassure themselves regarding three further considerations:

- Achieving objectives.
- Identifying the full costs and benefits of schemes.
- Risk analysis.

Achieving objectives

It remains critically important that the preferred option actually achieves the objectives assumed of the development strategy. Case Study 1 above provides a classic instance where assumed impacts can hide ultimate objectives. There can be a tendency to assess training programmes in terms of immediate impacts: numbers trained, jobs secured, and qualifications attained. However the anticipated impacts apparently arising from some options may appear less impressive when subject to more searching questions as:

- Are those who receive training those most likely to get jobs anyway?
- Do training schemes, and jobs which may flow from them, focus on problems faced by those most distanced from the labour markets?

- Is training necessary to get the jobs that are on offer?
- Are any jobs obtained by those undergoing training sustainable in the longer run?

Perhaps the key message from all of this is the critical importance of **defining accurate objectives**. An objective "to provide training in order to improve labour market opportunities for the economically inactive" is likely to garner general support across partners. However more explicit objectives make the whole process of defining options and selecting a preferred choice altogether more transparent. In this example for instance an alternative objective might be: "to provide customised training to 400 currently inactive residents in district x, of whom half will be women, and 25% from immigrant communities; this training will lead to 200 full-time job equivalents lasting at least one year, of which 100 will be in the healthcare sector."

Identifying the full costs and benefits of schemes

One of the mechanisms through which to help guide the choice of a preferred option is to carry out a **full** assessment of costs and benefits. This should be done as part of impact assessment. However there can be a tendency to look at impacts in rather a narrow fashion without fully identifying **all of the benefits** arising from different options.

Clearly the degree to which a full cost-benefit assessment might be carried out will vary across development strategies. In many instances impact analysis will point to a preferred option.

But where major developments are proposed it may make sense to put preferred options through a more rigorous assessment of the full benefits arising from options.

Considerations might include:

- Over what time period will benefits occur?
- Are there likely to be any **unplanned benefits**? For instance if training programmes are designed for women, is this likely to boost child-minding activities?
- What are the **distributional implications** of proposals? Some options may appear to create modest impacts, but will actually generate greater benefits to society as a whole in the longer run. Intensive training programmes which provide jobs for those marginalised from the labour market will ultimately bring greater rewards than will programmes focussing on those who are likely anyway to get back into work.

- Is the preferred option **sustainable**? It may be that a redevelopment programme based on new roads would be easier and cheaper to implement than one which put in place a dedicated light rail project. But which will be most sustainable in the long run?

Risk analysis

There is a well-known tendency for appraisals to be overly optimistic. This is not surprising. Agencies and key actors will want to see local development strategies agreed and implemented. Rigorous appraisal can be seen as inhibiting that process. Benefits can thus be assumed when it is by no means assured that they will actually occur.

Once a preferred option has been agreed there may therefore be a need to undertake an appropriate **risk analysis**. This is likely to consist of various elements including:

- A critical overview of both full costs and assumed benefits. What does the evidence base say about similar schemes elsewhere? There can be a tendency to underestimate costs and over-assess benefits.
- Are objectives and budgets plausible?
- Are some elements of the strategy dependent on factors beyond the control of partners?
- Is there an appropriate financial and legal basis to the preferred option? Is the funding in place? Could implementation face any legal challenges?
- Are key staff in place? Will there be any critical delays if "the right person" cannot be recruited? Are some elements of the strategy especially dependent on specialist skills? Are these in place?
- Does the management team seem appropriate? If the project requires a partnership of agencies and actors, is that in place? What would be the implications of some partners leaving the project? Are some absolutely essential, and if so, how can they be tied into the preferred option?
- Will any delays prove critical? For instance do some financial streams have to be spent within a particular time period?
- Has the scheme identified possible "escape routes" if problems occur? What is option "B"?

Finally too it will be important to consider unintended consequences. These can have a quite profound effect on development strategies. Some might prove beneficial. For instance programmes to create innovative firms might bring other players to the table, such as local universities. But sometimes unanticipated consequences can raise difficulties.

A new training programme might prove so "successful" that it puts other suppliers out of business. There are two key lessons here: monitoring and evaluation systems need to be in place through which to identify unintended consequences; and managers need to be given the freedom to move quickly in order to maximise beneficial, and moderate negative, effects.

In conclusion

This chapter has considered issues surrounding the identification and selection of options for local development strategies. Three key issues merit emphasis at this stage:

- For understandable reasons there has been far less emphasis on devising options than implementing strategies: as a process it has not received the attention it deserves.
- It need not necessarily be a complex process. Major projects will require a proportionate allocation of resources in order to identify plausible options, but for many schemes it can be a relatively straightforward exercise.
- But it is also a critically important activity because it opens up the possibility of selecting a preferred option which is much more likely to result in cost-effective solutions: an early commitment to devising and selecting options can pay for itself many times over in the longer run.

Identifying Options – Summary of Do's and Don'ts

Do's

- Make sure options reflect defined objectives.
- Take steps to make the overall process of defining and selecting options as transparent as possible.
- Ensure that the preferred option will achieve the desired outcomes.
- Make sure options address the needs of specific social groups.
- Insist that all key stakeholders have a role in defining and selecting options.
- Involve those often neglected actors and agencies: voluntary and community sectors and business.
- Insist that options consider questions of management and strategic governance.
- Make sure that options set out the full costs and benefits to society as a whole.
- Place sustainability at the centre of option selection.
- Accept that it may take a long time to achieve some outcomes.
- Remember that options need to have effective monitoring and evaluation systems in place.
- Be prepared to set up formal partnerships if that seems the best way to implement some options.
- Use the evidence base to assess options.

Don'ts

- Don't ignore the value of "doing nothing" – at least in the short run.
- Don't devise options which might help improve infrastructure but which don't address issues of social capital and innovation.
- Don't neglect the emerging issues of competitiveness, innovation and social capital.
- Don't be afraid of radical options.
- Don't just go with the tried and trusted.
- Don't ignore the views of key local, regional or national politicians.
- Don't forget to look at the risks involved in options.
- Don't forget that some more innovative options may need a plan "B" if things go wrong.

Chapter 3

Assessing Expected Impacts

by
Colin Wren

Assessing the expected impacts of proposed strategies is a difficult task because it involves projection into the future. This chapter offers guidance, drawing attention to the potential approaches and the advantages and difficulties involved. An initial choice needs to be made about whether to adopt simple or more sophisticated approaches. The sophistication of the assessment should increase with the scale and complexity of the strategy; the financial, time, data and human resources available; the degree of political demand, and; with the level of understanding of the user.

There are two main approaches available for **measuring** the expected effects it is possible to identify two main approaches:

- A "top-down" approach deals with effects at the aggregate market level, like industrial sectors, and focuses on impact in relation to global objectives.
- A "bottom-up" approach deals with effects at the individual agent level, and focuses on the outcome in relation to specific objectives.

Choices must also be made concerning assessment **criteria** and **indicators**. The assessment criteria are used for making the judgement, like efficiency, effectiveness. The indicators need to be chosen for the intermediate outcomes and impacts, which must be made in relation to the relevant objectives.

Ultimately, the assessment will collect data and other information on the expected effects, for the purpose of informing decision makers on the appropriate courses of action, both initially and ongoing. In some cases it is best just to set benchmarks by which to judge the future performance of a strategy, but in other cases sophisticated modelling may be undertaken.

Introduction

Assessment of expected impacts is a tool for improving the quality of economic development strategies. It provides information to decision makers with which to form judgements on the value of a local development strategy and to make choices between competing strategies. It gathers data and undertakes analyses for three related purposes:

- To help define the objectives and design the nature of an intervention.
- To ensure that the objectives can be met and that it is effective.
- To help set targets against which the intervention can later be evaluated.

The crucial data and information to be collected includes not only the costs of the strategy itself, but the benefits and costs that accrue to the local economy. These may occur years into the future, may impact either directly or indirectly, and may be intentional or even unintentional. Consistent with the purposes of strategic assessment, once collected, the uses to which the data and information on the expected impacts may be put are as follows:

- To choose between alternative policy options.
- To decide upon the right scale of expenditure.
- To set targets against which the policy can be monitored and evaluated.

These uses could relate to the local development strategy as a whole, or constituent elements making up such a strategy or programme, *i.e.* individual policy instruments. The options for a strategy were considered in Chapter 2, while the issue of monitoring is taken up in Chapter 6. The purpose of this chapter is to consider the measurement of the expected effects, in order to fulfil any or all of the above three purposes. Of course, the effects to be measured vary with the nature of the development strategy, and it is not possible to offer a definitive blueprint for all assessments. Rather this chapter offers a framework and guidance on how to go about measuring the effects of a local development strategy. It draws attention to the main features, and to the difficulties involved.

The different characteristics of a local development strategy were considered in Chapter 2, *e.g.* nature, purpose, financial and geographical scale. These determine the nature of the effects, while the assessment will also vary according to each of the following, which lead to a number of choices. The nature of these choices is considered in this chapter.

- The number and complementary nature of the **instruments** involved, *i.e.* single or multiple, and directed towards the same or different specific objectives.
- The **objective** or **targets** against which the assessment is being made, *e.g.* broad aims (raise an area's gross domestic product [GDP]) or specific objectives (*e.g.* increase the number of start-up firms).
- The **assessment criteria** being used to make the judgement to make the prior assessment, *e.g.* efficiency, effectiveness or cost-effectiveness.
- The **timeframe** of the strategy, *e.g.* a seven-year, five-year or even a single year programme.
- The economic and institutional **context** of the development strategy, *i.e.* stable or relatively unstable macro-economic or political conditions.
- The **resources** available for the assessment, including funding, time, data and the human resources in terms of their availability and skills.
- The **capacity** and understanding of the user of the assessment.

A framework for assessment

To fulfil the purposes of strategic assessment, the gathering of data and information on the expected effects should be carried out early on in the policy process, and prior to implementation, when the options are still open. For this reason it is known as prior assessment, *ex ante* evaluation or appraisal. It confronts the question of "what will happen?" This is different to the usual situation in *ex post* evaluation where this is known, and the issue of interest is "what would have happened?"

In order to carry out the prior assessment it is vital to have a framework. This must be constructed in the light of the objectives of the development strategy (Chapter 1), and it must make use of a "problem analysis" (European Commission, 2001). The "problem analysis" consists of an outline of the problem to be addressed by the strategy, the agents and factors involved and how these relate. This framework is primarily used to work out the nature of the development strategy, but it is useful to the assessment in identifying how the strategy is likely to have its impact. The features of a "problem analysis" are set out as follows (European Commission, 2001):

1. Define key aspects of the situation to be addressed by the programme.
2. Identify factors likely to influence the key problem.
3. Identify the main groups of actors that will be influenced.

4. Analyse the cause-and-effect relations between the factors identified and the interests and motivations of the actors.
5. Construct a visual representation of these relationships.

The "problem analysis" indicates the effects that are expected, and it draws attention to the causal relations that exist between the strategy and the effects. These relations can be explored in greater detail by using what is known as a "logic model". This shows the chain of expected cause and effect running from the strategy to the final (expected) impact of the development strategy.

The "logic model"

The "logic model" is presented in its barest form in Figure 3.1. To keep matters simple this is for a development strategy that involves a single policy instrument, *i.e.* a job creation scheme. Of course, the actual situation will inevitably be more complicated than this, but as an abstraction from reality, Figure 3.1 is useful for drawing out the main features.

Figure 3.1. **The "logic model"**

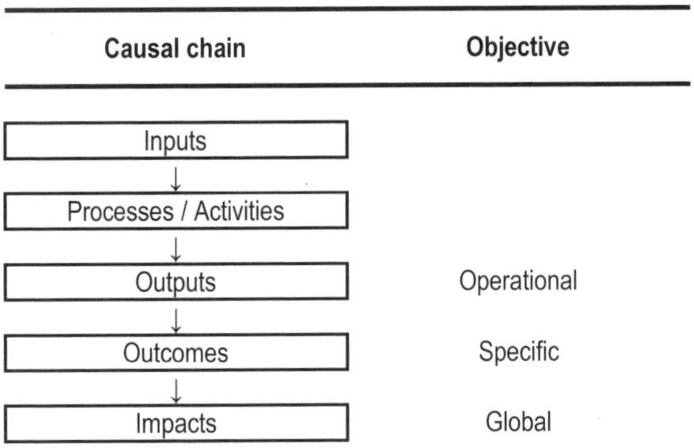

The precise use of terminology is important in evaluation, as misuse causes confusion. Figure 3.1 shows the chain of cause and effect running from the **input** to **output** to **outcome** and finally to the **impact**. The first two of these can be defined as follows:

- **Input**: The input **is** the intervention. It is usually measured in cost terms (*e.g.* the value of grants or cost of works to land), but it could be measured in other units, such as the hours of advisory support to develop entrepreneurship or hours of training to enhance worker or management skills.

- **Output**: The intervention generates outputs via a set of activities or processes. For a job creation scheme it is the increased number of jobs in supported firms. However, it could be the number of hectares that are developed or the number of individuals that are trained on a programme.

In general, the basic problem in evaluation (whether *ex ante* or *ex post*) is that not all of the **outputs** will be attributable to the intervention. For example, some (or perhaps even all) of the firms creating jobs may have created the jobs anyway, irrespective of the scheme. Further, there may be indirect effects that occur in other firms. For example, supported firms may put other non-assisted firms in the local area out of business. In this way it is also important to distinguish between the **outcomes** and **impacts**:

- **Outcome**: The outcome (or what is also sometimes known as the result) is the short-term effect experienced by the agents or markets directly affected by the strategy, *i.e.* over the first year or so. In the case of the job creation scheme it is the jobs in supported firms that would not have been created without the scheme.

- **Impact**: The impact is the longer-run economy-wide effect experienced by all agents or markets within the local area, *e.g.* over a period of two to five years. The impact includes the effects of the job creation scheme on other firms in the local area, including feedback effects on those firms that were initially supported by the scheme, so that matters can be quite complex.

This taxonomy points to some fundamental choices to be made in the assessment. One of these is whether to measure the expected effects in terms of the outcomes or in terms of the impacts.

The outcomes and impacts

Having outlined the chains of expected cause and effect running from the inputs to the impacts, it is necessary to decide on what data should be collected, and then how these data should then be analysed and interpreted. This involves collecting data on **indicators**. These indicators are considered in greater detail below and in Chapter 5. For now the level at which the indicators are chosen is considered, and hence at what level the data and information need to be collected. The "logic model" suggests the indicators can be defined at different levels, either in terms of outcomes or impacts, or indeed they may even be defined at the level of the inputs or outputs.

Consider the example of the job creation scheme. Table 3.1 illustrates different kinds of indicators. The **input indicators** capture the support given to firms, *e.g.* the grants taken up and administration costs, and the **output indicators** measure the results of this support, such as the number of firms or jobs supported. However, these are the gross jobs, and not all of these will depend on the support, so that the **outcome indicators** measure the number of net jobs that are attributable to the support. The **impact indicators** are defined in terms of the overall employment effect of the scheme on the local economy.

Table 3.1. **Indicators for a job creation scheme at different levels**

Level	Description	Possible indicators
Input	Grants and administration	Annual commitment of funds Annual payment of funds Administration costs
Output	Projects	Number of firms supported Gross jobs supported Firm compliance costs
Outcome	Jobs created	Net jobs created by firm Improved operating efficiency
Impact	Increase in employment	Net jobs created by economy Unintended effects elsewhere

In distinguishing between the output and the outcome the concept of "additionality" is important. This is the extent to which an intervention alters the behaviour of agents, such as in the timing, scale or nature of their activities. It could be that in the absence of government support all the jobs would otherwise be created by firms, so that the scheme has no effect, so it is said to be "non-additional". In this case, the outcome is zero, even though there are non-zero outputs. Where there is a zero outcome then the expenditure is said to represent "deadweight spending", and the jobs are referred to as "deadweight jobs" (see HM Treasury, 2002).

The **outcome** captures the short-run effect directly attributable to the intervention, *i.e.* the net jobs in firms. However, there may be longer-run effects in the supported firms induced by the intervention that require other outcome indicators to be defined. In Table 3.1 this is the improved operating efficiency of supported firms, which may cause them to generate even more jobs in the long run, but which are not otherwise captured.

The **impact** is the economy-wide effect occurring in the long run. In terms of Table 3.1 this is the increase in employment occurring throughout the local economy as a result of the scheme. It can be measured at the aggregate level, although this may be difficult if the scheme is relatively small, so that its effect is difficult to detect, or where aggregate data are not available or collected at the relevant local level.

If the indicators are defined in terms of outcomes and data collected for these, then it is important to realise that the measured effect of the development policy will in general not be the same as when the indicators are defined in terms of the impacts. This is because there are various **indirect effects**, and it will be necessary to collect data on these. Further, even if data are collected for the impact, it is useful to have knowledge of the indirect effects in order to understand how the policy works and to interpret the results. The nature of the indirect effects should be articulated in a "theory of action" considered below.

The indirect effects

There are essentially five kinds of indirect effects:

- **Displacement**: effects occurring elsewhere in the direct market.
- **Linkage**: effects in markets related to the direct market.
- **Feedback**: longer-run effects in the direct market arising from linkages.
- **Multiplier**: effects in subsequent periods arising from changes in factor incomes.
- **Externalities**: effects on other agents not transmitted via prices.

Displacement effects – This refers to the beneficial activities of other agents that no longer go ahead as a result of an intervention. These relate to the direct effect, *i.e.* the market in which the intervention occurs. In the case of Table 3.1, these are the jobs in non-assisted competitor firms that are lost because of the support. For example, the support could increase the demand for labour and cause a general wage effect in the local economy that displaces other workers. In the case of regional policy in Scotland, for example, it is estimated that the displacement jobs are substantial over the long run, amounting to one-quarter of the gross jobs created (see Gillespie *et al.*, 2001, on this issue).

Linkage effects – These are the economic linkages that exist between the agents affected by the intervention and the other agents in the local economy that may be affected over the longer run. These may take many forms, and it is a highly complex task to trace all these through in the economy. As a rule, it is useful to focus on the most important of these, by considering those agents or markets that are most closely related to the agents or markets in which the intervention takes place.

A distinction might be made between "vertical" effects in supplier firms and "horizontal" effects that occur via consumption. In the case of the former, if the strategy increases the output of supported firms then it will increase the sales of supplier firms (although displace the output of firms selling the same product or service). In the case of the latter, the intervention may increase the demand for "complementary" goods, but reduce it for "substitute" goods. For example, tourism support may increase the demand for rail or bus travel (complementary goods) but reduce it for other leisure activities (substitutes).

Feedback effects – These arise because the effects occurring in other markets may have knock-on effects on the agents directly affected by the intervention. It means the long-run direct effect could be different from the short-run direct effect once these feedback effects have occurred, but possibly greater or smaller. For example, if non-supported firms go out of business then this may have a positive feedback effect on supported firms by increasing the output price. Conversely, in the tourism example, the increase in demand for rail or bus travel increases the fares for these services, choking off demand for tourism.

Multiplier effects – These result from the increase in the incomes of the inputs engaged in producing the output generated by an intervention, such as the employees, managers, shareholders and owners of capital. Over time, and through successive rounds of what is known as the **multiplier process**, the income generates economic activity when it is spent in the local economy, *e.g.* individuals filling the new jobs spend their income on locally produced goods creating jobs in other activities. This leads to further rounds of the multiplier process as these recipients spend their income, and so on.

The multiplier is relevant for assessing the impact of large investments or closures (*e.g.* a car plant or shipyard) on a local economy, where in addition to the effects on supplier firms, there is a widespread boost or depressing effect on the economy from the gain or the loss of employment and income. The multiplier effects for many different kinds of intervention have been studied extensively (see Armstrong and Taylor, 2000).

The analysis of the multiplier process amounts to determining the **local multiplier**, from which the overall long-run multiplier effect is calculated. It places the greatest importance on the first round of the multiplier process (*i.e.* where the income directly generated by the intervention is spent). The key issue is the extent to which the extra income is either returned to the local economy or whether it leaks out. The **leakages** are likely to be greater, and hence the impact on the local area smaller, the:

- Smaller is the physical size of the local area and/or the size of its economy.
- More industrially specialised the area, so that the more it is reliant on goods and services produced elsewhere.

- More any increased taxation is used to fund national government services rather than returned to the local area.
- More in-commuting there is in the local labour market, so the benefits flow out.

Externalities – In addition to the above effects, there are other external effects. These are not transmitted through prices, but via by other processes, *e.g.* imitation, learning or transfer, and are known as externalities. They are particularly important for certain kinds of intervention. For example, a reason for attracting foreign investment is that it has beneficial effects on domestic firms from **spillovers**. These arise from the supposed better product and process technologies of foreign firms and their better organisational and managerial practices, etc., which may improve the competitiveness of local firms.

Choices regarding assessment

The nature, purpose and scale of a development strategy will determine the effects, and in addition, the introduction to this chapter noted that other factors affect the nature of assessment. This means that there are choices to be made, and important to these are the objectives against which the strategy is assessed and the criteria used to form the judgement on whether a strategy is worthwhile or not, and at what scale.

The objectives

The assessment should be made relative to the strategy objectives. These can be defined at different levels, corresponding to the impacts, outcomes and outputs shown in Figure 3.1. The European Commission (2000) offers a logical relationship between the objectives and the impacts, outcomes and outputs (see Figure 3.1):

- **Global objectives**: these give the overall strategy for the intervention.
- **Specific objectives**: these are the priority areas of the intervention.
- **Operational objectives**: the objectives of individual measures and instruments.

In the case of the example in Figure 3.1 the **global** objective is to increase the employment of an area. To achieve this it works through priority areas, which for this example is the **specific** objective of job creation. It is implemented through the **operational** objective, which are the grants to firms. There may be other priority areas and operational objectives in support of the same global objective. For example, a training scheme that improves labour market matching (operational and specific objectives respectively) could support the same global objective of increased employment.

The assessment criteria

The assessment criteria are the issues that the assessment seeks to address, and relate to its purpose. For a prior assessment the questions are **predictive** in nature – what will happen? – and **critical** – will the intervention effect the required change? According to Tavistock Institute with GHK and IRS (2003), the principal assessment criteria are:

- **Relevance** – To what extent are the objectives of the intervention relevant to the needs and priorities of the implementor? It relates to appraisal, and the choice of the best development strategy in order to achieve the objectives of policy.
- **Efficiency** – How will the inputs be turned into outputs or outcomes (see Figure 3.1), and can better results be achieved using fewer inputs? This involves comparing the effects achieved with the resources used.
- **Effectiveness** – How far will the strategy contribute to achieving the specific or global objectives? It considers whether the outcomes or impacts will meet the objectives, and issues such as what are the successes and difficulties.
- **Utility** – Will the programme have the desired impact on the target groups in relation to their needs? This assesses the effects in relation to broader societal and economic needs, including particular target groups, *e.g.* ethnic minorities.
- **Sustainability** – To what extent will the changes (or benefits) be expected to last after the intervention has been completed? This considers whether the outcomes and impacts are durable over time and after the intervention has ceased.

The assessment criteria are distinct concepts although not necessarily independent of one another, so that increased efficiency can lead to increased effectiveness, etc. Assessments may differ in the criteria that are applied. Taking the job creation outcome in Figure 3.1, efficiency is whether there are cheaper ways of creating jobs (or getting more jobs with the budget), while the effectiveness of support is how well the jobs created relate to the level of jobs that are required or planned.

"Top-down" or "bottom-up"

The choice concerning the appropriate objectives and assessment criteria must be made in conjunction with the assessment methodology. The latter is considered below and it has three elements: method of data collection; techniques for data analysis; and "tools" on which to base the recommendation or judgement.

Choices over the objectives, criteria and methodology essentially result in two kinds of assessment: "top-down" or "bottom-up". Again, these are not mutually exclusive. In deciding which of these to focus on the factors outlined in the introduction to this chapter are important, such as the purpose, instruments, timeframe, resources and capacity for the prior assessment. In either case, the assessment is made for a determined geographical area, that is at the local level. The key features of the two approaches are:

- **"Top-down" approach**: this kind of assessment is carried out using indicators and data for broad aggregates, *i.e.* the local economy as a whole. The global objective is relevant and the assessment will collect data on the impact, which will aggregate both direct and indirect effects, so it attempts to get at the long-run net effect. However, the approach is less good for determining the outcome, and in particular the contribution to the impact of the priority areas or instruments, *e.g.* how well job creation and labour training contribute to the global objective of increasing the employment of an area.
- **"Bottom-up" approach**: this considers the effects at the level of individual agents, *e.g.* firms, employees or households. For these kinds of evaluations, the focus is on the outcome, and the operational and specific objectives are relevant. In these approaches the indirect and longer-term effects are often ignored or are only roughly calculated, so that the impact is assumed to follow in due course. Thus, for example, we may know that a job creation scheme is likely to create a certain number of net new jobs, but not how these will impact on the employment of the local economy once the displacement, linkage, multiplier and feedback effects are taken into account.

In practice there is nothing to stop the assessment using both "top-down" and "bottom-up" approaches to measure the expected effects, although there may be a difficulty in reconciling the results. In the case of local development strategies a key issue is that the spatial scale or expenditure on the strategy may be relatively small, in which case it may difficult to detect the impact of the strategy from all the other changes affecting the local economy. Here, it may be best to focus on the outcomes.

Finally, assessments sometimes use a mixture of approaches. It is difficult to determine the **impact** from a "bottom-up" approach, as all the important linkages between agents must be identified and the expected effects must be measured, but sometimes a "top-down" assessment is used with aggregate-level data to examine the **outcome**. It is the case for the UK *ex post* evaluations of regional policy in the United Kingdom:

- The global objective of UK regional policy is to reduce over the long term the persistent gap in growth rates between the regions; and
- The specific objective of the main instrument of UK regional policy, regional investment grants, is to encourage sound projects, which improve employment opportunities.

Just about all the "bottom-up" evaluations evaluate the grants in terms of the specific objective, while the "top-down" assessments also focus on job creation, rather than the global objective.

Practical difficulties

The above discussion provides a framework for prior assessment and indicates some of the choices that must be made in these assessments. However, it is not without many difficulties and controversies. These are worth briefly looking at, as they serve to highlight the practical problems and some of the limitations of the framework outlined above. It leads to a discussion of the appropriate indicators.

The "black box" of evaluation

One criticism of the above approach is that it does not reveal much about the processes by which the effects are brought about. The approach may be fine where the purpose of evaluation is for accountability, but much less so where the purpose of evaluation is formative (see Introduction) and so about improved planning and performance. Referring to Figure 3.1, the approach views the intervention like a production process, with inputs yielding outputs. However, it reveals little about the processes yielding the outputs, and which as a result is sometimes known as the "black box" of evaluation.

An alternative is the **realist approach**, which has gained popularity in recent years. This argues that the focus of evaluation is the agents' own accounts of their perceptions, motivations and actions in order to understand the processes at work giving rise to the effects (Pawson, 2006). While there are different strands, a common feature is the need for the evaluator to work with the actors involved in the process in order to determine the mechanisms by which the desired outcomes are expected to arise.

While a traditional evaluation might reveal if an intervention is worthwhile or not, the realist approach might indicate how to improve the intervention, possibly in order to make it worthwhile. It is advocated for community economic development programmes, which embody a range of initiatives, but which place an emphasis on community engagement.

Systemic versus market failure

The indirect effects sketched above suggest a highly complex chain of cause and effect, even for a single instrument intervention. This is not least because the feedback and multiplier effects work through the system in complicated ways and at different speeds. Notwithstanding this, a criticism of the framework is that the environment in which the policy is applied may be subject to a **systemic failure**, rather than the **market failure** that is usually taken as a rationale for intervention (see Chapter 2).

Where a systemic failure exists then an intervention may only be as good as the weakest part of a system and possibly unsuccessful if there is a weakness or if it fails to connect with other development activities. The systemic failures are associated with research, technological development and innovation (RTDI) interventions. However, they may be relevant to some kinds of local development strategy that are multiple instrument interventions, and which fail to connect with key elements.

For RTDI interventions, an evaluation approach is proposed that is rooted in the realist tradition (Romanainen, 2004). It involves asking expert panels to provide qualitative assessments of the (prospective) impact of parallel interventions. However, it usually does not result in quantitative outcomes, while the "Evaluation Guide" prepared for the European Commission finds that the "evaluation methodologies have not been up to the task" (Tavistock Institute with GHK and IRS, 2003). Nevertheless, where the effects are of this kind, this approach could potentially be used in prior assessment.

The "theory of action"

As part of the prior assessment, it useful to have what is known as a "theory of action". This seeks to describe the likely or expected chain of cause and effect, and it could be drawn from either the positivist or realist tradition, or possibly both. The "logic model" in Figure 3.1 is a simplified "theory of action", but in general for any particular local development strategy it will be much more complicated than this.

The purpose of a "theory of action" is to describe the mechanisms by which the strategy is expected to have its effects (desired or otherwise). It is useful for:

- Identifying the global, specific and operational objectives.
- Determining the major effects, how these link and sources of interaction.
- Identifying the relevant indicators for which data need to be collected.
- Structuring and carrying out the assessment.

The "theory of action" is vital for carrying out a prior assessment, particularly those that are "bottom-up" in character, but also those that are "top-down". However, in practice, a "theory of action" is difficult to articulate, both due to the complex processes at work and the weak understanding of these. For example, many local development strategies have the global objective of increasing the GDP or growth rate of some area, but the factors contributing to economic growth, even at a national level, are not particularly well understood and subject to considerable debate.

In a similar vein, Baslé (2006) believes that the underlying weakness in the evaluation of the European Union development programmes is the poor articulation of a "reference model". The European Commission does not have a model of territorial action, while Baslé believes that improvements in this situation are reliant on developments in theory, accompanied by more detailed modelling and testing, in order to learn about the factors affecting local development. In fact, many agencies are fast developing a model of their economy (*e.g.* using an input-output model or computable general equilibrium model), and these can be used to develop a "theory of action" for a development strategy.

The indicators

No matter how imperfect, the "theory of action" can be used to determine the **metrics** for the prior assessment. This is the system of **indicators** on which data are collected, forming the information for the prior assessment. Information systems and monitoring data are discussed at length in Chapter 6, so that here the focus is on the concept of indicators. Indicators are useful for monitoring and *ex post* evaluation, but in the case of prior assessment they must be capable of being able to answer the **predictive** and **critical** questions identified above, *e.g.* what will happen as a result of the development strategy. The indicators must also capture objectives that are often vaguely expressed, *e.g.* an improvement in competitiveness.

Choice of indicators

Given the taxonomy of potential effects outlined in Figure 3.1 and associated objectives, it is clear that indicators can be selected at different levels, *i.e.* impact or outcome. Further, give the complexity of the effects it is possible that indicators may be defined at some intermediate level (see below). Overall, the choice of indicators will depend on the assessment strategy, which will in turn depend on the factors identified in the Introduction to this chapter, *i.e.* the nature of the development strategy itself, the resources available for assessment and the context in which the assessment is being undertaken. Here, we briefly outline the choice of the different kinds of indicator given in Table 3.1.

Impacts – The choice of indicators for the impacts seems relatively straightforward. If the global objective of the development strategy is to increase employment, then data should be collected for this. If it is to improve the relative growth rate of a local area then the appropriate indicators might be the GDP for this area and for comparable areas. This is illustrated by Table 3.2, which shows the impact indicators used by the UK government to benchmark its productivity objective (HM Treasury, 2004). This objective is adopted at the regional level by some agencies, and for regional interventions. It shows that data are collected on seven indicators, capturing different aspects of the objective.

Outcomes – This is associated with "bottom-up" evaluation approaches. In principle, the choice of indicators is straightforward, since like the impact and global objective, the outcome indicators can be defined in relation to the relevant specific objectives (Figure 3.1). However, like the impact, the outcome may occur years into the future, and this poses a particular problem for prior assessment given that it is *ex ante* in nature. For these indicators, it is useful to distinguish between **intermediate** and **final outcomes**.

An **intermediate outcome** is an outcome that occurs in the chain of "cause and effect" before the final outcome (or outcome). The intermediate outcome occurs sooner in time, but in the passage of time the expectation is that it will lead inevitably to the final outcome (and in turn to the impact). The link between an intermediate and a final outcome arises from the "theory of action" outlined above. Where the final outcome occurs years into the future, or is difficult to ascertain, then the prior assessment can focus on intermediate outcomes, and measure the expected effect of the strategy in terms of these.

Table 3.2. **Impact indicators for productivity objectives**

Public Service Agreement Target 1: Demonstrate progress by 2006 on the Government's long-term objective of raising the rate of UK productivity growth over the economic cycle, improving competitiveness and narrowing the productivity gap with the United States, France and Germany.	
Indicator 1	Trend rate of productivity growth (output per hour) over the last complete economic cycle
Indicator 2	GDP per worker – France (UK = 100)
Indicator 3	GDP per worker – Germany (UK = 100)
Indicator 4	GDP per worker – US (UK = 100)
Indicator 5	GDP per hour worked – France (UK = 100)
Indicator 6	GDP per hour worked – Germany (UK = 100)
Indicator 7	GDP per hour worked – US (UK = 100)

Source: HM Treasury (2004), "Productivity in the UK 5: Benchmarking UK Productivity Performance: A Consultation on Productivity Indicators", HM Treasury, London,
www.hm-treasury.gov.uk/consultations_and_legislation/productivity_indicators.

Intermediate indicators

To illustrate the use of intermediate indicators, Table 3.3 sets out the "priority areas" for the UK government's productivity objective. The UK's "theory of action" is that increased investment, innovation, skills, enterprise and competition will lead to improved productivity. These are referred to as the "drivers" of productivity, and represent specific objectives (see Figure 3.1).

Table 3.3 shows the intermediate outcomes in relation to each priority area. None of the indicators involves measuring productivity itself, even though this is the ultimate objective of policy.

Several intermediate outcomes might be defined in relation to the same final outcome, forming a chain of cause and effect from the output to the final outcome.

In general, some guidance on the choice of indicators is as follows (DTI, 1999):

- **Outcome indicators** will in general be much narrower than impact indicators, as they are trying to capture just the short-run direct effects.
- **Intermediate outcome indicators** should be used only for those causal links that can reasonably be expected to follow. Unintended effects are best ignored.

Table 3.3. **Intermediate outcome indicators for specific priority areas**

Productivity "priority areas"	Indicators
Investment	• Hurdle rates: required rate of return for a business to invest • Business investment as a % of GDP • Government investment as a % of GDP • Perceptions of the quality of infrastructure • Innovation
Innovation	• Publications and citations of research in academic journals • Business enterprise research and development as a % of GDP • Triadic patents: patents granted in the United States, and patents applied for in the European Union and Japan • Proportion of enterprises with co-operation arrangements on technological innovation activities with other enterprises or institutions
Skills	• International comparisons of the overall level of qualifications • Highest qualification of economically active adults in the United Kingdom • Business executive perceptions of management quality
Enterprise	• Fear of failure preventing people from starting a business • Venture capital investment as a % of GDP • Cost and time to register a firm • Total entrepreneurial activity • Difference between the productivity growth of small and medium-sized enterprises and of all firms
Competition	• Trade in goods and services as a % of GDP • Product market regulation • Competition regime peer review: a survey of competition experts relating to the effectiveness of the competition regime in different countries

Source: HM Treasury (2004), "Productivity in the UK 5: Benchmarking UK Productivity Performance: A Consultation on Productivity Indicators", HM Treasury, London, www.hm-treasury.gov.uk/consultations_and_legislation/productivity_indicators

- An intervention may have **several final outcomes** where it affects several markets, which may imply several chains of intermediate outcomes.
- An **identical set of indicators** need not be used to assess all interventions, but where relevant consistent indicators can be used to aid comparability.

The indicators need not be specific to an intervention, and may be chosen to aid comparison across different kinds of intervention, known as **core indicators**.

In practice, the choice of indicators depends on the understanding that the assessor has of the causal chain of effect going from the output to the impact, and on how far down this chain the prior assessment can reliably collect data and other information.

Assessment methodology

In conjunction with the objectives and assessment criteria, and in the light of the "theory of action", the assessment must decide on a methodology, which has three components:

- The method of data collection.
- The techniques for data analysis.
- The "tools" that are used to base the recommendation or judgement.

Again, there are many options, and these are shown in Table 3.4. The choice must be made according to whether the assessment is "top-down" or "bottom-up" and the indicators.

Table 3.4. **Types of methodology for prior assessment**

Methods of data collection	Techniques of data analysis	Tools to base judgements
Social surveys	Cross-tabulation and correlation analysis	Financial appraisal methods
Beneficiary surveys	Input-output analysis	Cost-benefit analysis
Individual (stakeholder) interviews	Econometric models (Computable General Equilibrium models)	Benchmarking
Priority evaluation	Regression analysis	Cost-effectiveness analysis
Focus groups	Shift-share analysis	Economic impact analysis
Case studies	Experimental / quasi-experimental approaches	Gender impact assessment
Participatory approaches and methods	Delphi survey	Environmental impact analysis
Use of secondary source data	Strengths and weaknesses analysis (SWOT)	Strategic environmental assessment
Use of administrative data	Net present value	Multi-criteria analysis
Observational techniques	Internal rate of return	Expert panels

Source: Adapted from Tavistock Institute with GHK and IRS (2003), *The Evaluation of Socio-Economic Development: The Guide*, Tavistock Institute, London.

In general, several kinds of methodology can be identified, varying in their level of sophistication and purpose, as follows:

- **Outputs and inputs**: the methodology could be simple, and involve little more than data collection on the expected outputs or even inputs, *e.g.* amount of industrial space provided, length of roads constructed or number of firms supported.
- **Impacts and outcomes**: more usefully, the methodology will seek to determine the likely effect of the strategy in terms of outcomes or impacts. For impacts it may involve using a formal model for the local area. For outcomes it involves collecting data on things such as the expected amount of net new development (*e.g.* from new industrial space or roads) or number of net new jobs.
- **Target setting**: the purpose of the assessment may be to set targets for which data can be collected, both for monitoring and for evaluation at a later date. The targets may be set relative to the outputs (*e.g.* number of training places) or the expected outcomes or impacts (*e.g.* number of trainees finding jobs or the level of employment in the local area).

Modelling approaches

Where there exists a suitable model of the local economy at an appropriate level, then it can be used to make an assessment of the likely impact. Broadly, there are a number of approaches that can be used to estimate the impact. These are technical in nature, including input-output analysis, macro-econometric methods and a computable general equilibrium model. Treyz and Treyz (2004) review these methods and their pros and cons. In the case of a local development strategy a key issue is whether the model can be constructed at the appropriate scale and whether aggregate data can also be obtained at this level. This potentially is a key constraint, which may limit the use of these models in local development strategies.

Treyz and Treyz also outline the REMI Policy Insight model, which seeks to combine elements of each of the above approaches into a single model. To date, the REMI model has mainly been used in the United States, but has found applications in Europe. The model can be constructed for a single region, for multi-regions (allowing for inter-regional linkage and feedback effects) or for a multi-regional national model.

Sources of information and data

In terms of the development strategy outcomes, and to support an aggregate-level analysis of impacts, it is necessary to collect data and information. There are a number of possible sources:

- Previous *ex post* or interim evaluations of similar strategies carried out in the local area.
- Previous evaluations of similar development strategies carried out in other local areas, possibly outside the region or country.
- Discussions with local agencies concerned with implementing the strategy.
- Contacts with sources of expert opinion, and
- Interviews with agents likely to be affected by the strategy.

In addition the assessment will collect primary data on the local area, or draw on other sources of data, published and unpublished. This will include data for the area as a whole (*e.g.* GDP or unemployment) and for agents (*e.g.* number of firms and employment), but which may also be in aggregative form.

Economic appraisal

In the case of appraisal there are well-developed tools on which to base the judgement. These tend to be rooted in the literature on economic appraisal, which is also known as **cost-benefit analysis**. Broadly, it involves collecting data on the benefits and costs that are expected to occur over time, and valuing these at their economic value or resource cost. Market prices give information on the economic value, although these may be deficient where markets are imperfect, for which "shadow" prices must be constructed.

For effects such as externalities, which do not have prices at all, these are valued using techniques such as **contingent valuation**. These techniques are pertinent to development strategies where the major benefits are improvements to visual amenity or reductions in travel times, for example transport infrastructure such as a road or bridge. Generally, economic appraisal will discount cash flows occurring over time to allow for the different time value of money. It also adopts a **net present value** appraisal rule.

Target setting and performance monitoring

A key part of the assessment of expected impacts should be to set targets for the local development strategy, for which data can be collected both for monitoring purposes and for interim and *ex post* evaluation. These not only inform future development strategies, but may lead to adjustments in the strategy itself if it is found to be substantially under- or over-performing.

In general, **monitoring** is the continuing process that involves the systematic collection of data on indicators in order to provide information on an ongoing intervention. It is used to check progress, and so differs from an evaluation, which is about the assessment of an intervention. It gives information on the progress and achievement of objectives, and progress in the use of allocated funds. The indicators chosen for monitoring can be of two types; they may just reflect changes directly connected to the intervention or they may check performance against a pre-determined targets or expected results, known as **performance indicators**. In the second case this is **performance monitoring**. It seeks to show results the relative to what was planned, so it involves setting a **benchmark** or collecting **baseline data**. These provide reference points or standards against which progress can be checked, but they differ:

- A **benchmark** offers a view on what can reasonably be expected to be achieved.
- A **baseline** records the position at the time that the intervention commences.

A benchmark is based on the performance that has been achieved elsewhere in the recent past or is coincident with the intervention, *e.g.* by comparable regions, countries or even agencies. In the case of a local development strategy it may be difficult to find suitable benchmarks, particularly where it involves a large number of instruments or the area is small or unique. In this case, it involves setting baselines.

A benchmark or baseline could be set in relation to the global or specific objectives (*e.g.* employment in the local area or jobs created by firms respectively in Figure 3.1), or even in terms of the outputs or inputs (*e.g.* number of supported jobs or the amount of public support). However, whatever they are, they mean data must be collected on the indicators as the strategy is implemented, representing monitoring.

Since many factors may affect the performance of a local area relative to the baseline or benchmarks, which are not explicitly controlled for, then performance monitoring may have little if anything to say about the impact of the strategy. Thus, it should not be seen as an alternative to *ex post* evaluation. This is carried out after the strategy has been implemented, for which the monitoring data may be a vital input.

Prior assessment in practice

Finally, it is possible to indicate further sources of practical advice on prior assessment. The first of these are the evaluations (*ex ante*, interim and *ex post*) carried out by the European Union on its economic development programmes. General guidance on evaluation procedures that emphasises and expands on many of the points made here can be found in Tavistock Institute with GHK and IRS (2003), while recent examples of different kinds of evaluation and problems therein of EU spatial development programmes can be found in Bachtler and Wren (2006). Further practical advice is found in the guidance for the evaluation of regeneration programmes issued in the United Kingdom by the UK government (ODPM, 2003). This approach is shown in Figure 3.2. It is based on the shorthand ROAMEF (rationale, objectives, appraisal, monitoring, evaluation and feedback) as a way of conveying the need for approaches that contribute towards the different stages of a policy cycle.

Perhaps the important point for policy makers is that the ROAMEF framework stresses the importance of feedback. It suggest that if local development strategy objectives can be devised explicitly as a continuous process of evaluator feedback, then the potential benefits for the efficacy of policy are likely to be substantial.

Conclusions

The purpose of this chapter has been to highlight the choices that must be made in assessing the expected benefits of a local development strategy and to demonstrate the different approaches to assessment that may be taken. Prior assessment is essential to ensure that the correct strategy is implemented and that the benefits are maximised for the local area. However, the choices that are made regarding the prior assessment will ultimately depend on the three key features outlined in the Introduction. These are the characteristics of the local development strategy (nature, purpose, financial and geographical scale); the available resources for assessment (funds, time, data and human resources); and the context in which the assessment is undertaken (economic, political and understanding of the user). Whatever approach is taken, a framework is required for assessing the effects, and part of the purpose of this chapter is to indicate the nature of such a framework.

Figure 3.2. **Stages of the assessment cycle within ROAMEF**

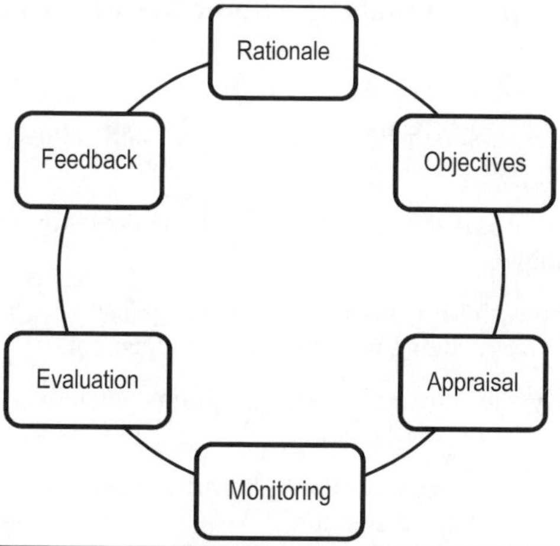

Evaluation	Appraisal
1) The definition of the problem: rationale, objectives and base lining	
Baseline conditions and counterfactual: What did the intervention seek to achieve?	Baseline and reference case comparison with objectives to define the problem
2) Defining alternative options/actions	
Characteristics of the intervention: What actions were taken? What alternatives were available? What would these have achieved?	Identification of options available to achieve the objectives
3) Identifying and measuring inputs (costs)	
What costs were incurred?	What will the options cost?
4) Identifying and measuring outputs and outcomes	
Examination of the changes that occurred	Examination of the likely impacts of the options
5) Results presentation and interpretation	
Did it achieve its aims? What worked and what was successful? Could more have been achieved?	Effectiveness of options in achieving objectives, risk, comparison with alternatives

Source: ODPM (2003)

Assessing Expected Impacts – Summary of Do's and Don'ts

Do's

- Commence the assessment in good time and allow sufficient time for its completion.
- Have a clear sense of the purpose of the local development strategy and what it is seeking to achieve.
- Be certain about the objectives or targets against which the assessment is to be made and the criteria being used to make a judgement.
- Try to identify the alternative policy options, including the possibility of doing nothing.
- Make sure the resources available for the assessment are adequate, including funding, data and human resources.
- Define the key aspects of the situation to be addressed by the programme.
- Identify the major expected economic, social and other benefits and the likely costs of the programme.
- Have a clear sense on the relevant indicators on intermediate and final effects for which data need to be collected and effects estimated.
- Be prepared to offer different estimates for different scales and alternative forms of the proposed intervention.

Don'ts

- Don't make the assessment over-sophisticated, but at a level that can inform decision makers and ensure an optimal decision is taken.
- Don't omit important expected effects, but at the same time don't spend excessive time on trivial effects that over-complicate the assessment.
- Don't carry out the assessment at an inappropriate spatial scale.
- Don't use methods and techniques that are inappropriate for the local development strategy under consideration.
- Don't ignore factors likely to influence the key problem, and the main groups of actors that are likely to be influenced.
- Don't ignore the possibility that matters will turn out differently than expected, so be prepared to present a range of estimates as key assumptions are varied.

References

Armstrong, H. and Taylor, J. (2000) *Regional Economics and Policy*, Third Edition, Blackwell: Oxford

Bachtler, J. and Wren, C. (2006) Evaluation of European Union Cohesion Policy: Research questions and policy challenges, *Regional Studies*, 40.2, 143-153

Baslé, M. (2006) Bonnes gouvernances publiques en Europe et évaluation. Introduction à un débat de socio-économie politique de l'évaluation, Économie publique, 10-2002/1. Put on line on 1 January 2006, http://economiepublique.revues.org/document508.html.

DTI (Department of Trade and Industry) (1999), "Guidance on Preparing Evaluation Plans", ES Central Evaluation Team, DTI, London.

European Commission (2000), "The Ex Ante Evaluation of the Structural Funds Interventions", Methodological Working Papers, No. 2, European Commission, Brussels, http://ec.europa.eu/regional_policy/sources/docoffic/working/sf2000b_en.htm.

European Commission (2001), "Ex Ante Evaluation: A Practical Guide for Preparing Proposals for Expenditure Programmes", Directorate-General Budget, European Commission, Brussels.

Gillespie, G., McGregor, P. G., Swales, J. K. and Yin, Y. P. (2001) The displacement and multiplier effects of regional selective assistance: a computable general equilibrium analysis, *Regional Studies*, 35.2, 125-139

HM Treasury (2002), "Appraisal and Evaluation in Central Government: Treasury Guidance", *The Green Book*, HM Treasury, London, www.hm-treasury.gov.uk/Economic_Data_and_Tools/Greenbook.

HM Treasury (2004), "Productivity in the UK 5: Benchmarking UK Productivity Performance: A Consultation on Productivity Indicators", HM Treasury, London, www.hm-treasury.gov.uk/consultations_and_legislation/productivity_indicators.

ODPM (2003), "Assessing the Impacts of Spatial Interventions, Regeneration, Renewal and Regional Development Main Guidance", Interdepartmental Group on the EGRUP Review, Office of the Deputy Prime Minister, London.

Pawson, R. (2006), *Evidence-Based Policy: A Realist Perspective*, Sage Publications, London.

Romanainen, J. (2004), "Learning More from Evaluations: The Use of the Thematic Approach and Impact Modelling in Evaluating Public Support Measures", European Conference on Good Practice in Research Evaluation and Indicators, University of Galway, Ireland.

Tavistock Institute with GHK and IRS (2003), *The Evaluation of Socio-Economic Development: The Guide*, Tavistock Institute, London.

Treyz, F. and Treyz, G. (2004) The evaluation of Programs aimed at local and regional development: methodology and twenty years of experience using REMI Policy Insight, ch. 6, 151-190 in OECD *Evaluating Local Economic and Employment Development: How to Assess What Works Among Programmes and Policies*, OECD: Paris.

Chapter 4

Making Use of Prior Assessment Results

by
Ville Valovirta

What difference a prior assessment can really make depends on various issues. At best it can bring about a better tailored and more coherent local development strategy, increase collective understanding about the means to attain goals and mobilise actors into contributing to the achievement of the goals. If it is not used properly, however, it might be a symbolic act with not much visible impact on how the local development policy evolves.

To ensure that the prior assessment of evidence leads to real improvements, it is critical that the results are used. This chapter examines how to do this, addressing how:

- The commitment of various stakeholders to prior assessment is an important prerequisite for success.
- The use of evaluation takes place in social interaction between various actors.
- The prior assessment exercise should aim to be a vehicle for collective learning.
- Involvement in the assessment process will have some impact on the thinking and behaviour of the people concerned, especially if participatory methods are used.
- How the results feed into the strategy process and other policy-making processes is of crucial importance.

Introduction

Making use of the results is the final step in an assessment process. It is easily thought to fall outside the evaluation process itself. Yet it is a crucial and integral part of the whole assessment process, since only if the results prove to be useful can an evaluation process be justified.

The perspective of use also provides us with a simple rule of thumb for deciding whether an evaluation is needed in the first place: the benefits of assessment should exceed its costs. Although this might not be easily calculated in advance, it certainly obliges one to think about the ways results should be used, by whom and when.

Making use of evaluation is seldom an automatic process. There exists ample evidence that evaluation studies are not always being utilised to a great extent, and that sometimes they are even simply ignored. This reminds us that one needs to pay attention to the issue of utilisation throughout the assessment process and plan the intended uses at the outset.

Prior assessments can be used in various ways:

- Conscious and **instrumental** use of results in revising the local development strategy following the conclusions and suggested policy recommendations.
- More **conceptual** use of results in gaining novel ideas, new perspectives and frameworks, or more nuanced understandings about the dynamics of local development.
- Using the evaluation process as an agent for **learning and change** among the stakeholders.

It is not only the results in the prior assessment or ex ante evaluation report that are being used. In fact, it is more likely to be the **assessment process** as a whole which generates the most profound impacts on actors' thinking and behaviour. The very process of carrying out an assessment is likely to influence the way a local development strategy will be adopted and deployed. It should also be remembered that it is people, not organisations, who use evaluation results. Therefore people who have an interest in the local development strategy and its outcomes are obvious candidates as potential evaluation users.

How can assessment results be used?

The ultimate goal of evaluation is to learn about local development strategies and the means of attaining strategic objectives. An ambitious evaluation scheme should aim explicitly at generating learning at individual, organisational and local levels.

Learning about a local development strategy can take several forms:

- Learning about strategic **policy goals**; what kind of development targets are worth pursuing on a local level.
- Learning about **policy instruments**; what works and in which context; which development approaches and tools can be used to attain the goals.
- Learning about the **strategy process**; how to prepare, design, manage and implement a local development process; how to commit various actors to it; how to communicate the expected benefits from engaging in the strategy formulation and implementation.

Learning is thus the ultimate target of evaluation. Evaluation can contribute to learning in the local development process basically through two functions: it can provide analytical evidence and arguments to strategy-making practitioners; and it can provide a process for interaction and reasoned debate between various actors.

Providing sound and credible arguments for policy making

First, the purpose of evaluation is to provide sound and credible evidence and arguments for a decision-making process. In some cases evaluation may bring up new information about the state of local development which affects the strategy choices. In other cases it may provide an alternative means of looking at the strategic options available and suggest a new path forward. Both evidence and the conclusions derived from it may be potentially useful for the local development strategy process. Prior assessment can:

- Clarify the rationale of the strategic objectives in terms of socio-economic development needs of the local community or the region.
- Sharpen the prioritisation of strategic goals, which often remain painfully vague and generic.
- Critically examine the relationships between policy measures, their outputs and expected outcomes.
- Impose more coherent logic on the development strategy (*i.e.* the "logic model" or "intervention logic" of the local development strategy).
- Assess the feasibility of the strategy in terms of its implementation plan.
- Provide a final "check point" before approving the action plan, thus making the justification for the planned expenditures firmer.

- Prior assessment can also function as "a critical voice". If legitimate rationale for interventions cannot be provided by evidence and analysis, a prior assessment should be able to suggest fundamental changes in the strategy. Or even more radically, refraining from taking action can be recommended if the case for intervention is not strong enough.

It needs to be recognised that evaluation does not bear automatic supremacy over other forms of policy-relevant information. Decision makers will always use their professional experience, common sense, intuition and tacit knowledge to form their opinion regarding the choices ahead of them. Various sources of information and deliberation will always play a great role.

Nevertheless, the results of a well-crafted prior assessment may offer more evidence-based analytical arguments than many other sources of information. In this respect, they are not just another source of information, but may provide balanced judgments on the basis of careful analysis of empirical data. One should not, however, assume too optimistically that evaluation will become the principal basis of decisions. Evaluators do not have a monopoly on knowledge. Evaluation is only one informational input among others in circulation, competing for attention.

Providing a process for interaction

A prior assessment should be seen as an elementary part of the local development strategy process. This is because it offers various **process benefits**. Even before the results of the analysis are finalised, the assessment process itself can already bring about many changes. It can:

- Build momentum, allowing managers and stakeholders to **reflect critically** on the strategic choices and presumptions about the dynamics of local development.
- Enhance understanding of the **drivers** of local economic development, such as innovation, learning, the adoption of new technology and entrepreneurship.
- Increase more informed understanding of the relations between activities, outputs and outcomes through an analysis of the strategy's **logic of interventions**. In real life, objectives and activities often get blurred. Carrying out single projects might become an end in itself, replacing the local economic and social development objectives the project was intended to serve. By linking planned activities explicitly to intended outcomes, prior assessment might help the local development strategy to stay tuned to serve the real development needs and problems.

- Strengthen **commitment** among the local decision makers and stakeholders. Simply being involved in the evaluation process and having the opportunity to express one's views to an evaluator might make people more engaged with the strategy process.

Process does matter. The use of a prior assessment, to a large extent, is relevant throughout the evaluation process, not only when the results are reported. Whether the assessment process can make a difference to the strategic choices depends largely on the measure of **interaction** between the evaluators and the stakeholders in the evaluation process. Participatory methods, which are widely used in assessing local development strategies, are powerful tools for reaping the full benefits of a prior assessment process. See Box 4.1, which illustrates the benefits of this process in Finland.

Utilisation of assessment results is not only about change in individual people's thinking and action. More importantly, it takes place in **social interaction** between various stakeholders – politicians, local government, business community, science and education institutions, voluntary organisations, media and citizens. How these actors individually and collectively react to evaluation results will determine its use. That is to say:

- How stakeholders interpret the meaning of prior assessment results; how the conclusions and recommendations fit with various actors' conceptions, ideas, expectations, objectives, interests, values and world views.
- How they discuss relevance and validity of the results in their respective organisations and various inter-organisational forums.
- How they negotiate the implications of an assessment of the strategic goal setting and its operationalisation into an action plan.
- What kind of decisions they will subsequently make to revise or modify the local development strategy and its action plan.
- How they will take the assessment results into account in their respective organisations during the strategy implementation phase.

The success of a local development strategy is largely determined by the commitment of various local actors to it. And this commitment will be created by repeated discussions and negotiations between the relevant parties. Consequently, a prior assessment will stand little chance of having significant influence on the strategy process if its results do not become a subject of discussion between the actors involved with the strategy.

Box 4.1. **Using a collaborative prior assessment method to promote learning in the Regional Centre Development Programme in Finland**

In the prior assessment of a development initiative in Finland, the local development strategies were studied with the help of a collaborative working method. The Regional Centre Development Programme builds on the idea of activating networking and co-operation between local and regional actors within local urban employment areas. The ultimate goal is to improve the competitiveness of the area by more deliberate strategic choices and commitment to commonly agreed objectives. The programme philosophy stresses the importance of local priority setting in the regions instead of top-down steering by national policy guidelines.

A significant element of the prior assessment exercise consisted of a series of evaluation workshops conducted in a participatory manner with local actors and stakeholders. The principal goal of these sessions was to clarify the logic behind the local development strategies. With the help of computer-assisted mapping of the strategy elements, the evaluation team aimed to make explicit the hidden assumptions about how intended outcomes are supposed to be attained. The purpose of this exercise was to achieve better understanding of the nature of the development strategies. The assessment of the strategies was designed to critically investigate the logical coherence and plausibility of the plan. It was also designed to build a foundation for intermediate and *ex post* evaluation in the later stages.

One of the tangible outputs of these collaborative sessions with local actors was visual illustrations – "strategy maps" as they were entitled by the evaluation team – which described the logic of the strategies through graphic presentations. In these exhibits, general level strategic goals and priorities, more specific objectives and practical measures were interlinked to form roadmaps for the local development strategies. These maps were combined with more detailed logical framework analysis including preliminary indicators and sources of monitoring data.

In light of the feedback collected from the participants, the interactive construction of the programme models provided an opportunity for learning about the strategies:

- The participants credited the workshops with helping them to obtain a more holistic and coherent picture of various actors' thinking.
- The goals and objectives of the local development strategies were discussed, modified and fine-tuned during the workshops. The mapping process clarified various levels of goals and revealed some inconsistencies, thus giving the participants a more structured model of the strategies.
- The mapping process also revealed discrepancies between the ultimate strategic objectives and the measures chosen for attaining the goals.
- The assessment process contributed in establishing indicators for monitoring the strategy.

The prior assessment thus contributed to creating shared understanding between operative actors about the local development initiative. Without a shared understanding of the programme's working model, it has limited chances of generating clear impacts. For a local development strategy to succeed, it will necessarily require the commitment of a multitude of actors. Therefore, a shared understanding about the nature of the programme is a necessary prerequisite for a local development strategy to have a significant influence.

Identifying the users

How can one ensure that a prior assessment of a local development strategy is given a chance to contribute positively to the strategy process and become utilised? The first step is to identify the potential users. This is needed because a local development strategy will most often be deployed by a network of several actors rather than a single local agency alone. Even if the strategy is intended to be implemented mainly by one single organisation, the complex dynamics of local development necessitates close interaction between various local actors in order to gencrate significant changes in local economic and social conditions.

Different types of actors have varying interests in the strategy process. Therefore it is useful to distinguish the main groups that are involved in a local development process.

Operative actors are those who possess resources (financial, human or intangible resources) to turn the strategy into action. These include regional and local authorities, education and research institutions, private companies and business associations, local civic associations, and various types of intermediary organisations such as technology transfer organisations. Since all these actors are likely to have differing expectations towards the local development strategy, their interest towards prior assessment is likely to vary accordingly.

Elected policy makers are those who are mandated to use representative democratic power to make decisions on local development. Their interest is often at a more general level than that of operative actors. However, their approval and commitment is often required for major changes to occur.

Finally, **citizens** also have a potential stake in evaluation as final beneficiaries of a successful local development strategy. They use their right to vote in regional or local elections and referendums (this naturally varies significantly between countries). Through democratic procedures they impose political accountability upon elected representatives.

All these groups of stakeholders are potentially interested in the results of prior assessments of local development strategies. Their interests vary, however. More general conclusions need to be communicated to elected policy makers and citizens, whereas the operative actors are more likely to focus on the more operative and technical matters related to implementing the strategy.

What can strategy managers do to increase the use of results?

There are several ways to improve the likelihood that a prior assessment will be useful for various actors. The organisers and managers of local development processes need to pay attention to the timing of the assessment, the means of communication and the means of managing complex networks of actors involved in the local strategy-making processes (Figure 4.1). More specifically:

- **Planning the expected use** at the outset of the evaluation process is one way to align the evaluation with its potential users' needs. One should anticipate the different ways that various stakeholders might use the results.
- **Timing** of the prior assessment is often also critical. The main results of the analysis need to be available when the major decisions are made. This does not mean, however, that a complete finished report need be provided to decision makers at the time of the decisions. Since schedules are often tight, it might be more realistic to require that the main findings and conclusions from the assessment will be formulated in a summarised form for decision-making purposes, and the complete report may be delivered later.
- **Targeted communication** to identified users is another means to increase utilisation. This should take place in several phases of the process. First, stakeholders should be informed about the evaluation study, its objectives and the schedule of when stakeholders will be expected to be engaged with the assessment process. Secondly, the stakeholders should be informed about how and when the results will be presented, and the implications for the development strategy.
- **Incorporating** assessment results into the strategy agenda is a natural step towards the utilisation of evaluation results. Too often all major decisions have already been made before the assessment results are available. This will leave evaluation with a largely symbolic and ritualistic role, with the possibility of achieving only minor modifications in the strategy.
- Mobilising **political support** from local policy makers is often necessary to ensure that evaluation has a chance to affect policy making. Politicians need to be informed about the process.
- An effective way to give evaluation more leverage is to engage a local **champion** – an influential local professional – in the evaluation process and in the use of the results in local policy making.

- Seeing evaluation as in part a **network management** tool might also help place it more effectively in a local development strategy process. Evaluation can be seen as one tool to provide increased "strategic policy intelligence" which could function as a platform for informed debate between various actors.

Figure 4.1. **What can strategy managers do to increase the use of results?**

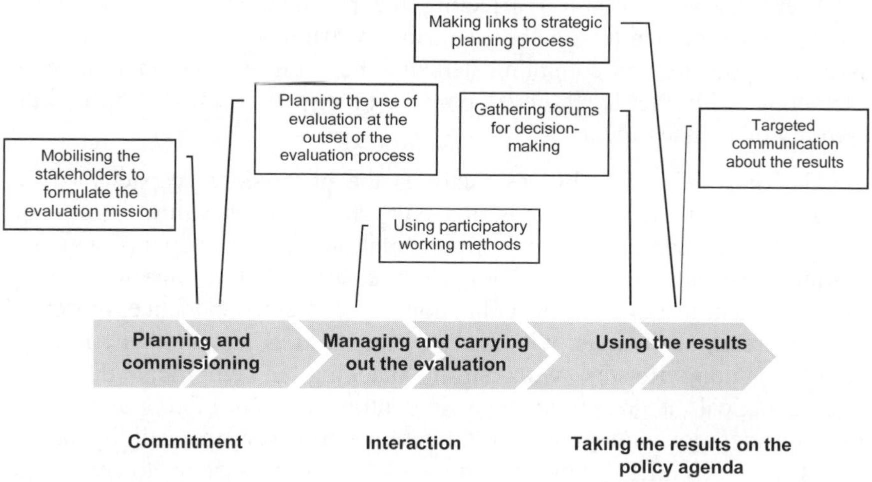

Promotion of discussion about evaluation results can take place at various levels. Strategy managers may actively promote the discussion on evaluation results:

- By putting them high up on the agenda of the strategy process.
- By inviting evaluators to present their findings in strategy workshops and allocating sufficient time for discussion.
- In some cases, it might be relevant even to promote discussion about the local development strategy process among local media to raise public debate about the goals and options.

It is not always easy to embed the evaluation process neatly in the evolving dynamics of a local development strategy process. Social scientists have discovered that the best window of opportunity for **policy change** is present when three interrelated processes converge: discussion about policy problems, agenda setting for solutions to these problems, and decision making at the political level. The local development strategy tries to channel these streams together into a coherent plan for change on a local level. Yet it might happen that the three processes evolve under diverging timeframes.

Thus the momentum for major changes to occur is not always automatically available, and needs to be created. To have a real impact on the policy, the main conclusions of evaluation should be brought up when the window for policy change is open.

What can evaluators do to increase the use of results?

There are several issues affecting the potential utility of evaluation which are determined by the choices made by evaluators. What methods are used, how results are communicated and how the evaluation process is interacting with the local development strategy process will affect the usability of an assessment.

The first and most obvious factor is the professional capacity of the evaluator to conduct a rigorous analysis which enjoys **sound and valid** credibility. Presenting sound argumentation where conclusions and recommendations are derived from robust data is a bottom line for making the assessment useful. A loose collection of fragmented evidence, presented in an impressionistic style, will easily be regarded as just another source of expert opinion. Results with strong backing in empirical data and methodological integrity in analysis, in contrast, are more likely to be taken into consideration and given due attention. However, the validity of the analysis in scientific standards does not merely suffice to make an assessment useful. The social, political and organisational usability of evaluation results will be to a large degree dictated by the dynamics of social interaction where evidence and arguments from assessment can be used for social purposes. This links back to the question of **relevance** – how does the prior assessment mission reflect stakeholders' needs and the specificities of the strategy process?

Evaluators can make their study more relevant to different actors by **negotiating the evaluation mission** carefully with the commissioners and stakeholders of the study with regards to their expectations and information needs. One of the common pitfalls an evaluator can make is not to clarify the programme managers' expectations about what can be learned from the evaluation.

An even more powerful way of providing potential benefits is to **involve local actors** in the assessment process. Local actors can be involved in several ways:

- Participation in **data collection** through face-to-face interviews and focus group interviews will provide them with opportunities to reflect on their expectations and offer a channel to feed their ideas into the strategy process.

- Collaborative working methods can also be used in the **analysis phase**. One may arrange expert panel meetings in which the implications of the prior assessment findings can be collectively interpreted and discussed. This may reveal unnoticed relations between issues or give insights into various types of constraints – be they political, financial, organisational, or cultural – which require closer attention.

- In the **reporting phase** the preliminary findings and conclusions can be submitted to key stakeholders for reality testing. Normally this takes the form of a draft report. But checking against the practitioners' experience may also take the form of an interactive "validation workshop", where additional policy relevance can be added by reasoned but critical debate on the possible strategic futures.

What evaluation users often value the most is a **new perspective** to look at the local development strategy. Those conducting prior assessments of local development strategies might need to find novel perspectives to look at the issues in order to bring further added value. A framework which establishes coherent and logical dependencies between various phenomena is often more useful than an analysis carried out strictly in line with regular ways of looking at local economic and social development.

Internal and external evaluators

Guidebooks on evaluation methods typically assume that evaluators operate as external experts in relation to the target being evaluated. The external status is generally assumed to permit a more independent, objective and credible position. Despite obvious benefits associated with the external status, it might in some cases be more reasonable to use an in-house evaluator, because:

- Using internal staff resources might be less costly than use of external experts (although this might be only an illusion created by fixed personnel costs).

- New knowledge produced by evaluation will stay inside the organisation and it might be better tapped into on later occasions, enabling organisational learning over time.

- An internal evaluator might be better equipped to act as an agent for change and a champion of evaluation use than external consultants or academics.

Also, various types of combinations of internal and external evaluators are possible. An evaluation design can be created where internal staff manage the process, collect core data and arrange interviews, workshops and seminars. Sometimes even preliminary analysis can be run by internal staff. The expertise of the external experts focuses on consulting on the design of the evaluation process, undertaking analysis and interpretation of the collected data, drawing key conclusions and reporting the results. The neutral status of an external evaluator may enhance the credibility of the results compared with a mere in-house assessment. Many of the aforementioned benefits of an in-house assessment can be accrued with a hybrid design. However, a risk remains that the assessment of the external experts remains superficial and dependent on the data provided.

It should be also noted that external experts may not always be neutral and independent *vis-à-vis* the local development strategy. Local universities, for instance, often have a strong interest in the local strategies. They are key stakeholders, carrying out research and development projects and education programmes, the financing of which may be subject to the local development strategy. As regards the role of the evaluator, discussion should not only concern formal contracting relationships between evaluator and the commissioner, but rather whether the evaluator has a "stake" in the local development strategy as one of the local partners or not.

Reporting evaluation results

There are many ways to increase the usability of evaluation by reporting and communicating the results effectively. Making an assessment is not only about producing a piece of policy analysis. It is also, to a great extent, a matter of communicating information and policy recommendations in effective ways. Some of the most significant factors in effective communication of the results of a prior assessment include the following:

- Use language which resonates well with the intended users' way of thinking and speaking. Avoiding technical jargon and specialist terminology will improve the likelihood that evaluation results have an influence.
- Present the results as complete arguments which logically interlink conclusions and recommendations with evidence and analysis.
- Illustrate the analysis with figures, charts, tables, and sometimes even pictures – it will make the report more informative and interesting.
- Use case examples from other regions or countries. Comparisons often represent more compelling knowledge to policy makers than a very detailed statistical analysis of one single local context without a point of reference. The power of examples, analogies and benchmarks should not be underestimated.

Targeting recommendations to separate audiences can also increase the likelihood that the outcomes of a prior assessment will be given due attention. Conclusions and policy recommendations can be differentiated to various stakeholder groups to match their level of interests:

- Strategic-level policy implications regarding the relevance of general goals and strategic choices should be mostly targeted at local policy makers.
- Questions concerning the feasibility of the plan should be the primary concern of operative actors.
- Questions about the strategy process itself are of interest to those responsible for designing and managing the strategy process.

It is often advisable to leave some room for the decision makers to do their job – that is to make decisions – by giving them a number of options rather than insisting on only one preferred strategy (Box 4.2 and Box 4.3).

Box 4.2. **Proposing several strategic options might be better than a single recommendation**

Policy makers can be forced to think in a more articulated way on their strategic choices if there are several options which link alternative goal settings with alternative actions. In the case of a local employment strategy, an evaluator might give several optional strategic recommendations, like the following:

1. If the main goal is to integrate young unemployed people into job markets through training and matching them more effectively with local small and medium-sized enterprises (SMEs), then "X" should be the preferred line of action.
2. If the ultimate target is to redirect local labour supply to better match the needs of local SMEs suffering from labour shortages, then the preferred strategy should be based on "Y" rather than "X".
3. If however, a more efficient balance between the two previous goals is being sought, you should choose "Z" which is also a combination of "X" and "Y".

It is commonplace that strategic goals remain vague. They need to be clarified by asking the policy makers for more detailed direction. However, it should be remembered that goals do not always get articulated first. Sometimes it is the means which have been decided first – and relevant problems are then identified to match them.

Nevertheless, giving several options should not be performed as an escape from valid analysis and sound argumentation. It is a way to leave room for policy makers to make reasoned choices between articulated options rather than restrict their room for manoeuvre.

In the complex political, economic and social context in which local development strategies are being formulated, there are always multiple options potentially available. Informed choices on these options can be assisted by providing alternatives with analysis of their full implications along various relevant dimensions.

Box 4.3. **Using scenarios to make proactive and anticipatory strategies**

A sophisticated way of offering strategic options is to test the strategic options in relation to a small number of scenarios. Scenarios are more or less plausible states of affairs imagined in the future. They are not intended to be predictions of the future, but rather equally plausible states of affairs evolving under different conditions and development trajectories.

Elements of scenarios are typically collected from various sources such as foresight studies, research reports, expert hearings and the like. Once scenarios have been constructed, all the strategic options available are then studied in each scenario. Looking at the strengths and weaknesses of the strategies *vis-à-vis* alternative future "worlds" might reveal factors which otherwise remained unnoticed. Putting the strategies in a "wind tunnel" of scenarios and testing their relevance can improve the analytic added value of prior assessment to decision makers. This can create more room for policy learning and prepare decision makers for better matching with alternative environments in the future.

Mobilising stakeholders to discuss evaluation results should be the main target of the utilisation process. In order to create discussion, the results of a prior assessment need to be supplied into the strategy process. This can be accomplished in the following ways:

- The most natural way to feed prior assessment results into the strategy process is to utilise **established co-operation processes and forums**. The local development strategy process should be designed to absorb new information and knowledge provided by the evaluation process.
- If existing forums are not available, special **evaluation results workshops** can be arranged. While being useful as such, they risk staying distant from the strategy making unless linked into the strategy process in a designed manner. It can sometimes be challenging to mobilise actors to attend meetings which have evaluation as the only item on the agenda.
- In some cases, the evaluator can play the role of a **facilitator** for joint discussion and decision making. This would naturally require that the evaluator possess facilitating skills. In the best case, it might create a bridge between the evaluation process and the local development strategy process.

- There are several **communication techniques** which may be used to promote the use of the results: slide presentations, long and short versions of the report, executive summaries, press releases, web communication material, etc.
- A separate **dissemination plan** can be made which specifies informational needs of various stakeholders and proper communication methods for reaching each respective group.

Where evaluation stops, the strategy process needs to continue. To make the link between these two is of utmost importance to making a useful assessment.

Cultural and ethical issues

There exists great cultural variation between nations with regard to how the role of an assessment is likely to be perceived by stakeholders of a local development strategy process:

- In some countries, it is widely accepted that external analyses are needed to provide feedback to development processes. People have learned about being assessed and they might have a genuine will to improve their policies and actions. An evaluation culture has evolved and been institutionalised into management practices. This facilitates embedding evaluation into a local development strategy process.
- In some countries with a legalistic tradition of public administration, evaluation might be conceived mainly as an activity of control. It can be associated with inspection and audit more than with learning and dialogue. In these contexts, more consideration needs to be given to clarifying the rationale behind the assessment and creating commitment to conducting it and using the results for improvement and learning.
- In countries with a long history under a communist regime, it might still not be culturally accepted that decisions made by local and regional policy makers will be debated and questioned by researchers or evaluation consultants. The transition towards a more reflexive culture in local administration might take a long time. Evaluation might contribute to changing the culture of administration towards transparency, collaboration and debate.

Evaluators need to adopt slightly different approaches in various environments. Cultural sensitivity and knowledge of the local context are virtues which help to cross the murky waters of local political tensions. However, one of the basic functions of evaluation is its role as an independent and external impulse to the local development process.

Therefore, too much sensitivity might make the whole effort meaningless if critical findings are being toned down. Clearly a balance needs to be found between "speaking truth to power" and maintaining cultural sensitivity.

Making Use of Results – Summary of Do's and Don'ts

Do's

- Find out what expectations various stakeholder groups have concerning a prior assessment study. Use their constructive potential for carrying out the mission.
- Weigh the potential costs of a professionally conducted evaluation study against its potential uses and make a judgment on whether the assessment will be justified from a cost-benefit perspective.
- Ensure that there is enough support from policy makers for carrying out and using the results of the analysis. If not, reconsider the added value from an assessment.
- Mobilise and involve stakeholders by formulating the evaluation mission and keep them informed about how the assessment process proceeds.
- Anticipate various forms of intended uses of the evaluation results at the outset of the process.
- Find an evaluator who carries credibility among the potential users.
- Plan the timing of the assessment to fit the local development strategy process in a way that the results will be available to be used in decision making.
- Encourage the use of participatory assessment methods, which will make it possible to reap the full benefits of the evaluation process itself.
- Write clear, concise and balanced reports where conclusions are justified with evidence and analysis.

Don'ts

- Don't assume that evaluation results will be automatically used for decision making by the mere provision of information.
- Organise forums for decision making if these are not yet made available by the strategy process.
- Carry out targeted communication regarding the evaluation results to various stakeholder groups: elected policy makers, operative actors, social partners and citizens.
- Don't rely only on a single written report; in addition, use face-to-face communication, customised presentations and executive summaries.
- If possible, try to make the evaluation report public and available for all interested parties to increase the transparency of the process and to promote utilisation of the results; make full use of Internet-based communication tools.

Chapter 5

Implementation of the Local Development Strategy

by
Neil MacCallum

This chapter considers the issues surrounding the successful implementation of a local development strategy. It underscores the importance of assessing, implementation issues and addressing them at the beginning of the process in order to embed implementation considerations in the development of the strategy and avoid some of the obstacles to success.

The chapter demonstrates the importance of establishing a framework for implementation and shares some thoughts on practical assistance for developing a transparent delivery process. The management methods and identification of responsibilities within this process are central to success. Leadership is crucial, as is a process that is inclusive and engaging across the partnership community. Commitment must be secured from organisations and individuals to perform and deliver within the timescales and resources available. Certain tools can then be applied to ensure this happens in the right way. The best use of such tools will depend on the local context, scale of the challenges being addressed in the strategy and the sophistication of partnership arrangements.

Introduction

All local development strategies start with a shared desire to deliver success and positive improvements in an area. In reality, many local strategies fail for a number of reasons, including poor implementation. Implementation is the crucial stage in bridging the space between objectives and outcomes. It is the practical demonstration of how objectives will be met in a timely way. This chapter considers this issue and how the obstacles to implementation can be overcome. A number of practical suggestions are made on how to ensure that implementation is considered and promoted **at the beginning** of the strategy development process and how to develop a learning culture within organisations and local communities.

Production of comprehensive guidance is important in delivering local development strategies and change in organisations and local communities. In theory, implementation should follow as a matter of course, yet it must be remembered that the materials provide a means to an end, **not** an end in themselves. In the end, it is the commitment of motivated people that delivers successful implementation.

Implementation is difficult. Nine out of ten strategies fail because of poor implementation. A local development strategy can look good in theory, but to be successful it must follow through at a practical level and consider the issues of implementation and the interplay of many small but often sensitive and significant local considerations. The local context is vital and obvious, yet many strategies give insufficient weight to the pivotal implementation issues which can become prime drivers, or barriers, to the success of the strategy.

Appraisal is about looking ahead and a local strategy must generate a shared view of what success will look like. This will also frame the appropriate measures to use in tracking progress and ensuring that evaluation is built into the strategy implementation process rather than be seen as something that is done as a bolt on at the end. Proper assessment of implementation issues at the outset can ensure that the strategy implementation process gathers evidence of effectiveness and efficiency as **part of the process** rather than retrospectively. If it is done retrospectively, meeting short-term targets often takes precedence over consistent commitment to the original vision and long-term objectives and thus compromises the ability to deliver sustainable change.

A proper assessment of the proposed strategy sets out the route for development, appraisal, approval and delivery of the strategy. Practical considerations must be prominent to ensure follow through happens successfully. As noted above, this sounds straightforward, yet it can encounter many risks, some of which are identified at the outset while other additional risks can emerge during implementation. This is especially the case if implementation issues are not considered as part of the overall strategy appraisal and planning process.

Planning is vital and an implementation plan should be an essential element at the strategy design stage. There are nonetheless a number of issues or obstacles that have to be addressed. These include:

- Implementation is difficult.
- The skills required are often not available locally.
- It can be difficult to attract key staff and long-term funding to support staff development and embed skills locally.
- The strength of leadership within the strategy partnership can vary. The most committed are not always the most powerful or influential to success.
- Political changes often alter the balance of power within partnerships and produce changes in policy or direction during the strategy implementation period.
- Being seen to act quickly often takes precedence over long-term commitment, especially if a budget is available for a finite period only and where there is insufficient clarity on how success can be sustained.

Establishing a framework for implementation

Every strategy requires a quality assurance framework within which implementation can be pursued successfully. This framework should set the context for action and have clear and transparent governance arrangements for effective appraisal, approval, delivery and tracking of interventions embodied within the development strategy and delivered through an implementation plan.

The framework should be of practical assistance to all staff, as well as stakeholders, in providing a transparent set of processes for delivery. This focus on delivery will ensure appropriate and effective actions to implement the strategy within agreed timescales and contribute to the organisation, partnership or community's ability to demonstrate the following:

- Achievement of fundamental goals.
- Intervention actions fit with strategy.
- Strategic contributions merit the priority of selected interventions.

- Focus on key drivers of growth and development.
- Value for money.
- Outcomes achieved and impact over time.

The framework should allow all appropriate actions to move swiftly from idea generation and appraisal to approval and implementation. At a management and reporting level, this should also allow the articulation of relationships between the various strands of the strategy, showing how the action interventions designed to deliver the strategy aims and objectives fit with relative contributions to the outcomes sought. Where the organisation or partnership is project- and programme-oriented, the development, implementation and management of the portfolio of actions should be treated as a core element in the strategy process. In this way, strategy management, budgetary control with risk assessment and project development decisions can be made clear. It will also demonstrate the important processes in governance arrangements and in skills and capacity development within a local community.

The framework should accommodate quantitative and qualitative performance measures or metrics. Where the local development strategy has a number of related themes and objectives to be delivered through a range of projects and partners, the organisation of information and its presentation can play an important role in communicating achievements and progress. Use of tools such as a version of the project logic chain, decision trees or balanced score card can be helpful. Such tools help to set out the relationships involved in the process of designing a strategy, including the role of implementation, and assist in preparation for evaluation and feedback of learning. By following a framework approach, a series of key questions can be addressed to allow an organisation or partnership to generate the detail relevant to its local development context. The benefits will include clarity on the following:

- Articulation of the relationships between strategy, operational plans, action activities and the delivery of measurable outputs, outcomes and impacts.
- The elements and key mechanisms for transmitting strategic intent into a productive portfolio of action projects, programmes and supporting activities that focus on the drivers of development and change.
- Integration of interventions to identify individual and joint contributions towards strategic objectives such that local actions can be linked to wider policy aims.

- Structuring of information, data and commentary, to improve accountability and provide an audit trail to show value for money.
- Budget control and resource allocation decision processes in line with accountability requirements for the expenditure of public funds.
- Business unit and partner management and prioritisation in line with the strategy such that projects, programmes and actions are driven by strategic objectives.
- Managing the project's life cycle to ensure focus on appraisal (at the start) and learning (at the end) to produce a clear rationale for doing more or doing less of certain activities within the context of the strategy.
- Driving change in organisations, partnerships and communities with regular reporting and performance updates to provide feedback on strategy implementation and achievements.
- Regular reviews and communications on a monthly or quarterly basis.
- Adjustments to reflect learning on performance delivery, requirements for further guidance and training, information and communications technology (ICT), management information, property and other support infrastructure.
- Ability to adjust emphasis as stakeholder or economic context factors change.
- Gathering of learning and building organisational and community memory.

Management methodology and responsibilities

The methodology for delivering the projects and programmes within the strategy should also be clear. Systems will be required for smooth management and delivery of an implementation plan within the terms of the overall strategy and the different aspects of appraisal (links between actions and outcomes, benefits and costs, responsibilities of actors – economic, financial, environmental, reputational, risk appraisal, etc).

Where the strategy is implemented in a top-down manner, agreed governance arrangements will be required to ensure that issues around the scale, novelty and risk should be clarified in the management process, identifying the extent of delegated authorities and localised decision making to make commitments on behalf of the organisation, partnership or community. Where the strategy is more bottom-up and local actors are also at the sharp end of the delivery process, the implementation will be less formal and more integrated and in such a context it is especially important to ensure that responsibilities are clear. In addition, it will also be important to harness energy and enthusiasm to develop capacity and capabilities at a local level for sustainable change to take hold.

In large organisations and partnerships, relevant processes for identifying "senior responsible owners" will be required, with approvals linked to future reporting arrangements that ensure the tracking of achievements over time, sharing of learning and ability to adjust operations as required. This will ensure that key decision makers and the leadership of the organisation are directly accountable for the implementation.

There is a need to avoid any concerns emerging around the planning and budgetary process. Projects being implemented should be devised and driven by truly strategic objectives rather than presented in a way that is seen to fit with the flexibility and scope built in to the strategy. The balance between doing the right things for the right reasons and just doing what fits and spends the budget is a very real issue in practice. The key question to ask is "are we doing the right things or are we doing things right?"

Safeguards will be required to be put in place to counter the risk of just doing things right. It is essential that things are done right but this should be related to the lead consideration of doing the right things. A key issue relates to the need for leadership. Leadership is required at a number of levels to ensure effective implementation. In devising the strategy development process and signing up for its implementation, the development executive and community representatives have the lead responsibility to take this forward within the organisational partnership as well as across partner and community organisations.

Implementation does not happen automatically; it requires drive and demonstration from leaders to motivate and mobilise appropriate behaviours throughout the organisations and community. Within lead executive organisations, senior management must present a clear commitment to deliver the strategy and put in place the methodology to achieve this in a consensual and inclusive manner. Links from the strategy to the operating plan and existing local plans are important in this regard.

Following preparation of the strategy, an "operating plan" process should ensure that projects and programmes are generated in line with the strategic priorities. Such a planning process should cover the short, medium and long term. The strategy and its effective delivery will emerge over time and it can take several years for an impact to occur.

There is a pragmatic requirement to produce indicators of progress in advance of impact measurement. The operating plan will cover the medium term (say three years) and annual plans will manage short-term activities. This relationship goes beyond the implementation framework issues mentioned earlier, to cover the spectrum of issues from inputs to impacts as discussed in Chapter 3 of this handbook.

Chapter 3 discussed some of the issues surrounding the logical model (from inputs, to outputs, to outcomes, to impacts) and the difficulty of attributing specific effects to a specific intervention. The logical and realist approaches described in Chapter 3 share the need to work with the actors involved in the implementation of the local strategy interventions in order to identify causes and effects and the various learning loops that occur within the project team and the local community.

It is essential to set out how the local development strategy will progress and how this will be evaluated to show impacts in the long term. In the short term, inputs and activities are likely to be the easiest to estimate and these will form the focus of appraisal and monitoring arrangements and statements can be made on the economy of actions. However, many appraisals fail because they do not go beyond such considerations to cover medium-term outputs and the efficiency of delivery.

Further, consideration at the prior assessment stage of evaluation of effectiveness and long-term impacts is often missing due to the difficulties in doing this, and often the lack of skills to do it locally. Good prior assessment requires that all these stages are covered and that learning is seen as part of the community development process and longer term skills capacity building which is in itself often an objective of the strategy.

At the outset, it is important to summarise the main elements of the strategy to be pursued using this methodology and state how the lead organisations and local actors will actually make a difference if it is implemented successfully.

This means being clear to all staff, stakeholders and partnership actors about the following questions:

- What is our focus – what improvements are we trying to affect?
- How will we deliver this – priority issues and initiatives?
- What are the appropriate measures of progress – what are the benchmarks and comparators?
- Where do we stand currently in terms of the key challenges being addressed in the strategy – a SWOT (strengths, weaknesses, opportunities and threats) analysis that shows the extent of the gaps to be filled?

- What are the operating principles in terms of how we will engage with customers and partners?
- What is our role in terms of the appropriate types of interventions and investments that will deliver the desired change?
- What are the guiding principles of operation expected from all staff and demonstrated by senior staff commitment?
- Do we have the processes in place to facilitate strategy implementation, including budgetary and resource allocations, ICT, staff skills development and training, approval processes for decision making including local delegated authority levels?
- What are the relative factors affecting flexibility of approach across a territory to take account of factors such as geography, industry and other issues, such as the social and political context?
- How we will track delivery and report progress regularly?

An integrated strategic operation is a key element of successful implementation in a co-ordinated and effective manner (Table 5.1).

Implementing the strategy can be aided with the assistance of specific tools within the methodology that illustrate the linkages between strategic vision and desired achievements. This can be especially helpful for internal operational staff in organisations and also for bringing clarity to partnership working. It also allows the ongoing review of a portfolio of interventions to check appropriateness and manage implementation. Where necessary, interventions can be altered and the portfolio mix for implementation adjusted. The approach can be applied at varying levels of detail from the very local development strategy implemented in its own context to a strategy that links into the regional and national multi-partner strategies. The approach allows for the expansion of the range and portfolio of projects if strategic focus alters, for example in line with stakeholder policy changes and in response to local changes and shocks to the economy.

As a disciplined tool, the approach allows executive staff and volunteers to operate consistently and summarise core implementation activity. Recording of this information in a systematic and searchable way, through a bespoke database and knowledge management system or standard ICT solution, will improve the key data, information and knowledge for the effective management of strategy implementation. Such an approach allows the partners flexibility to respond to changes and challenges, yet maintain the focus to achieve the desired impacts. It also allows formative and summative forms of evaluation evidence to be gathered in a complementary way. The strategic operations approach shown in Table 5.1 can evolve over

Table 5.1. **Integrated strategic operations**

Strategy development and implementation	• Focus on objectives • Leadership and commitment • Partners and communication • Identifying success factors • Tracking and reporting responsibilities
Operational alignment	• Clear roles and responsibilities to deliver • Complementary objectives for interconnected roles • Review of resource availability • Drive for outcomes shown by key performance indicators (KPIs)
Resource assessment	• Sharing resources with partners • Identifying key skills and gaps • Budgetary profiles and forward planning • Allocation agreements based on priorities and outcomes • Driven by returns not distributions
Intervention programme	• Appraisal criteria to determine actions • Formal guidance and governance materials signed • Monitoring methods for future decisions • Flexibility for effectiveness not expenditure targets
Feedback learning loops	• Processes for generating new ideas and pipeline projects • Reviews form a baseline and at milestones • Self evaluation and benchmarking • Recognising capabilities and capacity development • Triple tracking: project, people, product
Strategy review	• Recognisable outcomes and formalizing achievements • Progress defined by frameworks approach • Learning of lessons recorded and shared • Strategy refresh and adjustment of resources • Decisions based on impact

Source: Scottish Enterprise

time and assist communities and organisations (especially large formal implementation agencies) **beyond** the defined period of the strategy. This can be important as many impacts emerge beyond the strategy implementation period and require some longitudinal tracking to reveal the legacy effects. However the real challenge is to apply this approach without unnecessary bureaucracy and complexity.

Roles and responsibilities

Roles and responsibilities will vary according to the operational arrangements and the specific context of the strategy. In a small scale localised context, individuals often take on a number of roles in contrast to larger, regionally integrated development processes where more complex management systems may be put in place. In all cases, there should be transparent processes to facilitate the fast and efficient implementation of the strategy. Such processes and operating arrangements should also recognise the responsibilities attached to each role. In more complex cases, an agreed management and approvals process will be required. Liaison mechanisms should be established within the lead organisation (for example between the strategy directorate or corporate support and operations) to ensure focus and assist in the interpretation of strategic intent and contribution to delivering against agreed objectives. In smaller initiatives, and especially community-focused development, the learning gained from performing specific strategy implementation roles should be recognised as **part of the social capital** that is generated. The entire process can also act as a means of addressing development issues around a range of considerations including:

- Appraisal processes.
- Option assessment and prioritisation.
- Measurement approaches to gauge progress.
- Appropriate key performance indicators (KPIS).
- Reporting arrangements to community groups, senior management, board, ministers over time.

This applies to all levels of initiative although greater complexity will be expected for more integrated, high-cost and high-risk initiatives. For large, top-down development initiatives, a formal knowledge management system can be helpful for monitoring implementation at regular intervals and answering the basic questions, *e.g.* are we making progress as planned, on time and within budget? Self evaluation and peer reviews are especially important in bottom-up strategies where the capture of learning and knowledge is vital for long-term sustainable success.

The organisation or partnership should agree on individual board members as “champions” for strategic themes and key areas of intervention. For large initiatives, individual directors should then be identified to take direct responsibility for particular strategic objectives. In such cases, at the next level of management, senior responsible owners (SROs) should be identified for programmes or major projects. The SROs will work with functional heads and staff to draw together resources required to implement each area of the strategy successfully.

At each level, there should be a clear understanding of individual roles and requirements to report on actions and achievements. There should be clear guidance on the timetable and milestones for this, set within the approvals process. This again reinforces SMART principles (be specific, measurable, achievable, relevant, time-bound as defined by the UK Treasury) and in all cases it will be important to agree a baseline from which to measure activity and progress. This process should be a means of ensuring that management arrangements are in place and there is a route for tracking of achievements against the strategy. It is clear that in most cases the local development context will not require such extensive resource levels and management support. There are many good examples of local development strategies that have been implemented very effectively and efficiently without elaborate structures detailing precise roles, responsibilities and arrangements for decision making. However, every initiative will require clarity on the responsibilities of actors and the regular lines of reporting. Appropriate structures can be agreed between participants and reassurance gained by addressing a few basic questions including:

- Is there a clear connection between the strategic and operational planning processes ("Plans are not important, planning *is*." – General Eisenhower)?
- Do we have stakeholder and partner alignment within the agreed timetable and resources available?
- Do we have the budget and other resources available and can we get approvals for partner contributions in place on time or do we need to reprioritise?
- Are project documents and project plans clear for delivery of the strategy?
- Can we access and assess basic data and performance information for trends and insights?
- Are we able to measure contribution, understand connections between initiatives and identify any unintended consequences and impacts?

Local management arrangements should be in place to cover these points within the overall development framework approach. For larger initiatives, organisational management within each functional directorate and all operational staff should be clear on the extent of acceptable activity and the limits to delegated authorities to avoid issues of resource constraint or over-committing the organisation. Governance and controls are an essential element to shape behaviours and ensure alignment of individual actions. This will strengthen the links between strategy, operations and actions from the top and also from the bottom-up as individuals accept the responsibility in a way that stretches the organisation, community or partnership and the possibilities of the strategy itself. This should create a form of dynamic energy that finds a balance suitable for the strategic context and the key delivery priorities. In this way, a development culture emerges whereby individuals and organisations work together, accepting the wider appreciation of a shared responsibility for delivering the strategy that stretches from local operations to senior executive champions in organisations.

Obstacles to success

There is no simple model of organisation that will deliver success. It is the interaction of the combined resources, including skilled people, processes and technology, within an appropriate system that will create the dynamic necessary for successful implementation. At a small-scale local level, close relationships can produce a very effective model for implementation. Challenges often emerge in attempting to scale up such a model. As complexity increases with ambition and risk, bureaucracy expands and organisational structures can become difficult and costly to control. In such a context, agreeing the strategy and priority areas for intervention, identifying performance measurements and financial control systems, then aligning staff to utilise these systems is just the beginning. Some of the issues that arise and create obstacles to success include:

- Culture within the organisation.
- Confidence and skills of staff.
- Support to staff.
- Expertise available internally.
- Governance arrangements and bureaucracy.
- Guidance materials and their suitability.
- Politics internally.
- Personnel available.
- Capacity of the organisation.
- Resources available.
- Others.

Overcoming the obstacles

The combination, nature and extent of the obstacles will vary between organisations. However there are likely to be elements of some or all of the above in every context. In anticipation of such obstacles it is important to pre-empt events by promoting the following:

- A positive "can do" culture within the organisation.
- Generate confidence in the ability to deliver and the talent available within existing staff, partnerships and the wider community.
- Publicise the support available to staff in terms of leadership backing, training and development, ICT, rewards and incentives.
- Highlight specific skills and experts available internally and how to access their knowledge and experience.
- Emphasise non-bureaucratic systems that will help staff to do the job, rather than impede their delivery actions, and allow scope for extending the boundaries for innovative ideas that will deliver high-impact results quickly.
- Availability of quality, straightforward guidance written in a language that is friendly to the user rather than over-technical or patronising. Also ensure different types of materials are available in different formats to suit individuals with different levels of skills and experience as well as different learning styles.
- Leadership behaviours should be consistent and robust in dealing with internal tensions in a way that reinforces loyalty to the aims and objectives of the strategy.
- Staff development plans and prospects of accessing other additional resources as appropriate to ensure that the required personnel are available when needed.
- Confidence that the organisation has the capacity to deliver before setting out.
- Confidence that the resources will be made available and statements of support and commitment from partners, stakeholders, customers and commentators.
- Open channels of communication to pick up feedback and emerging issues within the culture of the organisation and a promise to act and report on the actions taken in response to any issues raised.

Box 5.1. **Hawick and Eyemouth, Scotland**

Hawick and Eyemouth are two small towns in Scotland which set up local strategic initiatives aligned with area and regional strategies. This rural area has a combined catchment population of around 20 000 people. The initiatives looked to co-ordinate inter-agency resources, build community confidence and capacity, help to deliver community economic development and small-scale infrastructure projects.

The five themes of the local strategy followed the five themes of the regional strategy. The communities created theme groups and theme leaders involving volunteers from within the settlements and a small committee provided direction and co-ordination of suggested project initiatives. An executive staff offered guidance and technical assistance although operations were devolved to a series of local project-related groups. The initiatives were positively evaluated in 2004.

The evaluation stated that in the absence of the partnerships, the implementation of the regional strategy and other publicly funded projects would be severely undermined. Some areas for improvement included the need to improve awareness of partnership activities, share success stories, identify succession strategies for themes not ready to **go it alone**, reduce bureaucracy and clarify the roles and activities of partnership. Other learning included the issue that some theme activities appeared to conflict with one another, especially where the disbursement of budget and changes in personnel were influencing factors. Further lessons were identified on issues surrounding reporting arrangements across different agencies and funders, clarity on monitoring to ensure that outputs are linked to the appropriate principal project and the need for a baseline measure of community capacity or confidence.

Source: Scottish Enterprise (2004), "Area Regeneration in Hawick and Eyemouth".

All too often, local development strategies are prepared in isolation from, or in competition with, the strategies of neighbouring localities, regions and the national context. Many also fail to focus on the key drivers of growth and development. Such local strategies that are implemented in competition with neighbours are likely to result in diseconomies and inhibit long-term growth and development. Co-operation rather than competition is the way to capture synergies, generate scale benefits and deliver sustainable improvements. Individual local strategies have often been promoted as successful, yet evaluation at a later date reveals the difficulties in achieving sustainable success if the strategy has not been linked to other strategic initiatives in the surrounding localities and region. Where a local strategy has been implemented in isolation, it will be important to address a number of actions including the following:

- Promote and communicate the local strategy – tell the community and others about the strategy and its implementation.

- Identify and engage with neighbouring area representatives and related policy initiatives – open a dialogue to explain the local context for the strategy and further development possibilities.
- Share the lessons learned from the local strategy development and implementation process – what worked well, what had the most influence on the key drivers of change, how was it resourced, how will the evaluated link back to the prior assessment.
- Discuss possible links and collaboration opportunities – how can synergies be created with other strategies locally, regionally and nationally and what will this mean for individual local strategies.
- Forecast the future benefits post implementation and further benefits that could be created from possible collaboration, transfer or scaling up, or ending of the local strategy by linking with wider initiatives.

Such considerations highlight the difficult choices that will face local development strategies and the importance of linking into other initiatives. There are examples where this has been achieved successfully (Box 5.1 and Box 5.2).

Though it is never possible to cover all eventualities, there are several core elements and principles of an implementation plan that can be put in place to guide activities, overcome likely barriers and draw upon the learning mentioned above.

Core principles and elements of an implementation plan

An implementation plan is an essential, integral part of the overall strategy process. It will ensure that everyone is aware of the responsibilities in delivering the strategy through a series of activities within a defined time period. The implementation plan will also drive the monitoring of strategy delivery and the future evaluation of the strategy process and its achievements.

The key principles of an implementation plan include the need to:

- Establish a process that allows for development as part of the strategy rather than as a bolt-on plan. Chapter 4 examined the issues around providing a process for interaction and the process benefits are a central part of the gains from implementation. An interactive process facilitates such gains which in turn generate the momentum for successful delivery.

Box 5.2. **City of Smolyn local economic development strategy 2004-07, Smolyn, Bulgaria**

Smolyn is located in southern Bulgaria and had a population of 47 500 in 2001. The area faced several challenges including a declining and aging population and high levels of unemployment. The municipality comprised 8 local councils and 86 towns and villages. The city formed part of the Cities of Change Program in the central and eastern Europe region, supported by the World Bank and the Bertelsmann Foundation.

The local strategy implementation plan developed a set of projects relevant to the strategy objectives, outputs and outcomes. Some were brought forward as ideas, some as feasibility studies and others as part of ongoing activities. Projects were then assessed against available budgets and then against selection criteria for inclusion in a Multiyear Investment Plan using a series of templates to produce a project score and ranking for priority of implementation. The recommendation for decision makers was informed by six points:

- Proposal of the criteria based mostly on the city strategy.
- Methodology of project's evaluation and selection.
- Proposal from content of project application forms.
- Step-by-step description of the process.
- Procedure of a workflow with a calendar of responsibilities.
- Review of the project application and proposed ranking of projects to be included in the plan for next year.

Projects were then moved forward to the Multiyear Investment Program Commission for decision with monitoring and review details including measures for post-implementation evaluation.

Source: City of Smolyn (2004), "Local Economic Development Strategy 2004-07", Smolyn Municipal Government.

- Ensure clear articulation of what needs to be done, by whom and by when in order to deliver the strategy vision, objectives, priorities and individual activities. Chapter 4 also identified how this can sharpen recognition of the importance of interventions and their sequencing.
- Define leadership and supporting roles for delivery elements of the strategy and service elements such as consultation, communications and public promotion. This can consolidate and unify commitment.
- The plan's structure should follow the SMART approach.
- Responsibilities should be agreed and all participants should share the determination to deliver the strategy with the resources available.

- An inclusive approach should be pursued to involve staff, stakeholders, community, customers, other organisations, press and opinion formers as well as ensuring representation from industry, academia and government.
- Use baselines, benchmarks and milestones (as discussed in Chapter 3) to provide a roadmap for action and progress.
- Identify the key risks to implementation and use tools such as a risk register to set out the risk appetite; also, decide on the priority risk response areas and options for mitigation, especially for the mission-critical areas of the strategy.
- Publish the implementation plan as part of the strategy to reinforce ownership and promote transparency.
- Allow space to accommodate input from others and ability to respond to shocks or unforeseen influences, including changes in the operational or political context.

A number of these principles are highlighted in the example below of how to define an implementation plan (Box 5.3).

Implementation planning and management

All organisations require a capacity or readiness for change. Where this is lacking, it will have a negative impact on the strategy implementation process. The position should be assessed and resources aligned to address capability and capacity issues. This has implications for management and staff roles and the assessment should underpin change management and training initiatives introduced before and during the strategy implementation process.

Good practice guidance materials and ongoing training and staff development are essential intrinsic components of successful implementation. As is promotion of a "can do" attitude, renewed visions of success along the way, backed with evidence showing updated examples of what worked and profiles of successful implementation. Enlightened organisations may take an integrated approach to such matters and involve staff in the gathering and dissemination of materials that act to inspire confidence and encourage consistent appraisal behaviours over the life of the strategy process.

Box 5.3. **Defining an implementation plan, an example from the United Kingdom**

Define structure – an implementation plan can take a number of forms. The product may depend to a significant extent on what other stakeholders need or want. The more specific a plan can be, the better. As a minimum an implementation plan should be clear about who is responsible for delivering what, by when.

Define the outputs/recommendations and the tasks required for implementation – clarifying what is required and breaking this down into specific actions. For example any single conclusion from a project may lead to a range of outcomes, a number of specified outputs, and many clear activities and deliverables. The aim should be to define specific, measurable, achievable, realistic and timed (SMART) tasks.

Define the milestones – be clear about the critical outputs and outcomes and the key milestones to achieving them.

Define the sequence – some tasks and outputs may be inter-dependent. It is important to map out the inter-dependencies and ensure that tasks and events are properly sequenced.

Clarify and agree responsibilities – the process of designing and agreeing an implementation plan can form a key component of the overall objective of securing stakeholder buy-in. Ultimately the responsibilities for delivering tasks should be clear and agreed by all key stakeholders.

Identify potential risks to delivery – there are likely to be risks to the delivery of the strategy. By conducting a risk-mapping exercise, to identify the likelihood and impact of potential risks, plans can be put in place to mitigate any high-probability, high-impact risks.

Be clear about the monitoring and evaluation arrangements – part of the implementation planning process should consider what success might look like. A plan might specify success criteria and key issues and mechanisms for monitoring and measuring progress; alternatively a plan could be clear about the need for the lead department to design a monitoring and evaluation framework within a specified timetable.

Document agreements – the process of putting together an implementation plan, and securing agreement from key stakeholders, will be critical in ensuring that conclusions are put into practice. The outcome of this process should be written up and shared with stakeholders as a document through which further progress can be monitored and chased.

Source: UK Prime Minister's Office, Strategy Unit, "Strategy Survival Guide".

Sources of implementation management guidance exist and the best is tailored to the needs of the organisation. Some countries have a set process that is used for major projects, strategic investment and procurement decisions.

The implementation plan for the strategy (and individual project plans) should identify clearly:

- A succinct statement of project or programme objectives for the intervention.
- How they will be delivered.
- The main risks to successful delivery and how they will be managed, including options for mitigating actions.
- Resources planned and required in terms of finance, personnel, equipment and partnerships.
- Who the project manager and senior responsible owner for delivering the project or programme, in whole and in its constituent parts, are.
- A timetable for delivery with key milestone dates for outputs and review dates.
- Mechanisms for tracking performance and incorporating learning and good practice. This is discussed in further detail in Chapter 6.

Implementation management for larger local development strategies should address a number of specific practical considerations as follows:

- Clear, rationale and SMART objectives setting out the timeframe for implementation and how to recognise when to exit successfully.
- Clear lines of reporting and decision making agreed.
- Stakeholders and partners identified with agreed terms of engagement, including board representation where appropriate, and means of conflict resolution.
- Project management framework in place covering:
    - Formal project plans including phases of delivery.
    - Use of a recognised project management tool such as PRINCE (**PR**ojects **IN** a **C**ontrolled **E**nvironment).
    - Project documentation and application procedures in place.
    - Baselines, benchmarks and milestones identified for measuring progress.
    - Expenditure and costs set out in the plan.
    - Data tracking and KPIs in place and capable of capturing required management information.

- Risk register that is reviewed and updated regularly with responsibility for ownership and management of risks allocated to individuals.
- Financial reporting arrangements linked into contractual commitments and organisational reporting cycles.
- Forecasts and targets set to link inputs to outputs with regular review dates and consideration for quality of outputs against an agreed specification.
- Procedures for tracking partner contributions, performance and dispute resolution.
- Compliance issues such as state aid considerations.

PRINCE is a process-based approach for project management developed by the UK Office of Government Commerce and is now recognised as an international standard. It sets out the principles of good project management that can be summarised as:

- A project will have a definite start and end within a finite process.
- Management is necessary for a project to be successful.
- All parties must be committed to success, recognising their respective roles and responsibilities.

Implementation reviews can ensure that effective delivery is happening, that appropriate governance and control processes are in place to report on performance and analyse variances. They can also check that planned targets and benefits are on track and risks are managed. Such reviews can be useful where a strategy embodies many projects or programmes being delivered over a period of years with several reviews being possible over the period of implementation. A review could be carried out by a group of peers from within the local community or organisations(s) or by an external review team. A report would then be prepared identifying named individuals with responsibility for following up on specific actions identified. In cases of complex or controversial initiatives, external facilitators are recommended for independence and objectivity. The implementation review process should focus on how to develop better projects with better delivery, within the context of the strategy. In practice this should mean less reliance on tight procedures and thus more emphasis on roles and responsibilities with individuals being empowered to apply judgement and experience.

Clear processes and good project and programme management are central to the delivery of strategy objectives and staff require the necessary skills and understanding to design and deliver projects and programmes successfully. The local context for each strategy (including scale of ambition, risk, complexity, range of interventions, etc.) will set the tone for the appropriate balance between governance and guidance. Principles of clarity, consistency and connection are relevant here. These principles applied to the implementation mix of projects and programmes will lead to **a route map** for the implementation process itself. By generating this process internally, the community or organisation can have a head start towards successful implementation and overcoming the obstacles to success mentioned earlier.

The route map can be reinforced by facilitation, animation, guidance and training. Indeed this is often essential where there is a lack of suitable skilled people in a locality. A training and development programme for actors in the community and support staff can be built around the principles of successful and sustainable strategy implementation. The style of training and mode of delivery can include contact and engagement to develop trust and a shared sense of purpose; presentations, practical workshops and role playing; written materials and online guidance, including self-assessment materials. The guidance should be consistent with, and appropriate to, the local context and local governance levels (including clear levels of delegated authority). In some cases, such as the example from Scotland in Box 5.1, volunteers from the local community can act as theme champions for an area of the local strategy and a local committee can be empowered to take operational responsibility. Public agencies providing resources should put in place appropriate support executives and management advice to facilitate the development process. Links can also be built in to access other information and guidance sources as well as **developing networks** between local actors and between areas and agencies.

A series of "how to" guides, workbooks, templates and checklists can be useful and made readily accessible on the Internet. These can be used to develop the stories of success and experiences to be shared with others in an open learning environment. Discussion can evolve and develop to form communities of practice. Communities of practice can become powerful vehicles for cultural change and maintenance of good appraisal in delivery of the development strategy. They are also a means of identifying **mentors and experts** to consult on specific topics. Experienced practitioners can be engaged to assist or mentor colleagues and such experience is invaluable in reconciling potential challenges such as linking resource allocation and strategy aims. Trainers, professional bodies and chambers of commerce can play an important role in devising appropriate materials and training programmes. Such programmes require targeting at the needs of individuals rather than attempt to train everyone in everything.

The detail of implementation must sit within an overall logical, clear and confident framework for implementation. There are examples where the strategy and its implementation have been devised after learning from what did not work in previous approaches. The World Bank has been prominent in sharing learning and successful approaches, especially with transition economies. One example of such learning comes from the Municipality of Lezha in Albania. Albania has a strategy for local economic development in various municipalities under the consistent framework of the Developing Enterprise Locally through Techniques and Alliances (DELTA) programme, supported by the World Bank, SOROS and FLAG. The goal of the programme is to develop strategic action plans that will have an impact on the restructuring of local economic development policies at the municipal level, especially those relating to the development of the private sector.

The development and implementation of the strategy for Lezha recognised that Albania was now open to international and national competition for attracting business and creating jobs. The mayor and his team in Lezha realised that the local development strategy required a clearer direction, focus and management of available resources. Previous efforts to attract economic activity into the area had been disparate, uncoordinated, unfocused and largely unsuccessful. Local initiatives had been competing and not linked to regional and national strategies. At the same time inadequate investment in basic infrastructure, poor physical environment, lack of supporting services and poor governance and financial incentives all compounded the inability to implement a successful local development strategy.

This did however lead to a refocusing effort around small and medium-sized enterprises (SMEs) as the driver of wealth creation, employment and sustainable growth in the long term. To devise and implement a local strategy based on this realisation required a new approach, new working practices and functioning partnerships, new involvement with the community, leadership and reliable local governance and a sense of civic pride. The resultant strategic planning process was part of the new approach and took 16 months. The planning process produced a new foundation for action by establishing:

- A professional assessment of the local economic base and the factors affecting local development.
- Agreement to actively review these factors.
- An understanding of the opportunities for growth and obstacles to local development.
- SWOT analysis to co-ordinate sustainable actions.
- Review of human and natural resources available.

- Recognition of the importance of local history, heritage, competitive advantages and needs of the community.
- Acceptance that local leadership is essential in accepting responsibility for implementation in the medium term.
- Acknowledgement that development must balance economic, community and quality of life issues.
- Implementation must be pursued in a holistic integrated process.
- The locality must protect and support businesses that already exist as well as attract new enterprises.
- Only a systemic approach can ensure consensus of the community and generate a common vision for co-ordinated effort.

The strategy was published in 2006 ("Strategic Plan for Economic Development", Municipality of Lezha, May 2006). It was recognised that the timeframe for implementation is longer than the political mandate and therefore guarantees will be required for project funding, consistent governance and continuous engagement. This was put in place alongside monitoring arrangements to produce quarterly and annual implementation reviews. A commission has been set up to allow revision of the implementation plan as required and local groups can be appointed to assist with assessing emerging issues.

This is an example of an implementation approach that has followed on from the commitments made during a detailed and inclusive strategy development process. It also grew out of learning from previous mistakes.

Conclusions

There will always be obstacles to success and this chapter discussed ways of identifying and overcoming barriers to successful implementation. This requires vigilance and it is important to link local strategy implementation to other strategic initiatives locally, regionally and nationally. Availability of skills locally to deliver an implementation plan and an integrated series of operational projects is always an issue and it is important to see the strategy implementation process as part of the local learning and capacity building effort.

Such an approach will build cumulative learning and allow lessons to be shared at a practical and strategic level to secure sustainable change. For this to happen, it is important to focus delivery efforts on the key drivers of growth and change. Several case study examples have been presented from around the world to illustrate aspects of the implementation process and to highlight learning that can be applied in a practical way to other local development strategies.

Implementation issues are central to the entire strategy development and delivery process. As such, strategy development must ensure that the details of implementation are considered seriously in advance of action. This is best done in a structured, co-operative manner using the approach, principles and tools described in this chapter. Central to this is the preparation of an implementation strategy and practical framework that sets out clear roles and responsibilities rooted within the agreed aims and objectives of the local development strategy.

Implementation of the Strategy – Summary of Do's and Don'ts

Do's

- Communicate clearly and devise a clear implementation plan that links local actions to the strategic goals.
- Have strong commitment and leadership, such that senior management "walk the talk".
- Have clear measures that demonstrate progress towards achievement of strategic objectives through an operating plan as well as delivering robust projects and programmes.
- Have review milestones and progress measures defined within the implementation and management plan.
- Report progress, encouraging and rewarding good behaviour, and impose sanctions for inappropriate behaviour to ensure accountability at all levels in the organisation or partnership.
- Conduct regular checks to ensure a focus on things that drive economic development and change.
- Recycle learning and establish communities of practice to encourage a culture that buys in to the strategy
- Ensure that partner's actions are aligned, as the whole is greater than the sum of its parts; demonstrate how local actions contribute to the delivery of wider strategic objectives.
- Demonstrate how implementation delivers change through people, process and projects.

Don'ts

- Don't think that everyone is a strategist and/or try to turn everyone into a strategist.
- Don't stifle innovation and flexibility.
- Don't undervalue experience against theory.
- Don't make processes overcomplicated.
- Don't have frequent changes of performance metrics (measurements).
- Don't raise expectations of short-term impact, yet don't avoid the issues of measuring contribution.
- Don't underestimate the importance of skills development and training.
- Don't allow a gap to grow between strategic and public relations messages on the one hand and staff, customer and stakeholder understanding and commitment on the other: There must be a shared vision and co-ordinated action to gain momentum for achieving the desired change.

Chapter 6
Information Systems

by
Jaime Del Castillo and Silke Haarich

Information systems are the backbone of the monitoring and evaluation systems that critically support the process of local development.

Setting up an information system starts with establishing links with the strategy design and delivery. Key partners to strategy must be involved as well as other relevant stakeholders.

Development of the information system must be integrated with the process of strategy building and delivery. Information systems need to be linked to key assessment activities prior to, during and after strategy delivery, including baseline studies, assessments of needs, and establishing results.

Professional information systems need specific technical support, but it may be more important to create a feasible and useful information system that facilitates basic data and conclusions on project activities, outputs and results, rather than having a comprehensive, but overly complex data storage system in place, without the capacity to analyse or use the data correctly.

When building information systems, one needs to take into account demand for different types of information and identify appropriate sources for respective categories of indicators.

Introduction

Functional information and monitoring systems are key features of any effective assessment and evaluation process for strategy development and implementation, this being true for prior assessment as well as for ongoing and *ex post* evaluation. A system of information defined to assess the policy objectives and management arrangements requires that:

1. The objectives and their priority status are clearly stated.
2. A definition exists of how those objectives are to be measured before, during and after policy or programme start-up.
3. A definition of the way this data is to be obtained exists, ensuring the availability of such data in each stage of the process.
4. Planning the technical, human and material resources required for monitoring and evaluation is done.
5. An efficient instrument is available to correct the orientation of measures clearly unsuited to achieving the objectives in good time.

Unfortunately, there is no such thing as a blueprint for information systems. Local or regional development strategies often require their own information systems and approaches and dimensions can vary considerably. Factors such as the number and type of stakeholders; information needs of stakeholders; evaluation requirements or other mandatory reporting mechanisms; availability of budget and human resources for technical assistance, monitoring and evaluation; experience and legal frameworks will influence the design, size and specific functions of information systems across countries, regions and policy sectors.

Nonetheless, some general guidelines may be defined on the effective creation and functioning of information systems in the wider framework of a local development strategy.

In this chapter we discuss the following questions:

- When and how to set up an information system?
- What to monitor?
- How to find and collect monitoring data?
- What to do with all the data?

Setting up an information system

The process of setting up an information system is essentially linked to the process of strategic planning and evaluation. Developing and implementing an effective and functional information system depends on the level of understanding of the linkages between programming, implementation, monitoring, evaluation, revision and feedback.

Information systems help to strengthen the capacity of relevant stakeholders to manage local development strategies, programmes and projects and to support decision making.

A good information system will provide information at the initial stages of local strategy development, by providing the baseline data for the programming and planning process. In the course of the programme implementation, information systems help to gather relevant information to support the assessment processes to identify specific improvements.

Monitoring information – links with project design, planning and evaluation

Defining and implementing a monitoring or information system should be physically, conceptually and operationally linked to the design and definition of a local development strategy.

Possible exceptions from this crucial linkage of monitoring and programming activities are, for instance:

- The setting up of a local development strategy by an institution or organisation that already has an institution-wide or local information system or monitoring and evaluation unit in place.
- The development of a programme or project with specific information and monitoring requirements and obligations. These need to establish the steps to be taken when providing information about programme progress, results and expenditure. Although in this case an information system is put in place, it may be limited to fulfilling a data production and control function, while rarely creating any benefit for the efficiency and effectiveness of the development strategy itself, since it is not linked to the programme development cycle or to general learning and feedback loops within programme management. One example of this might be the compulsory monitoring and evaluation systems put in place for the financial management and control of European Union Structural Fund programmes, as is the case of the computer programme FONDOS 2000, for the European Regional Development Fund (ERDF) in Spain (funding period 2000-06), which facilitates supervision and

control of financial execution, but is not conceived to offer the information needed for analysing the efficiency and effectiveness of programmes financed by those funds.

- The (late) development of an information system for an already existing and partially implemented development strategy. From a long-term perspective and with regard to future programmes, this could be a constructive measure, although it may lead to incomplete data analysis and evaluation for a given development strategy.

There are various links between programme design and implementation, and monitoring and evaluation, corresponding to subsequent information needs. If the objectives and accompanying measures are clearly defined, the variables enabling them to be monitored may also be clearly defined. Once these variables have been defined, the measures may be implemented and the data to be used in their subsequent evaluation compiled simultaneously.

The prior assessment stage in particular is where specific links between programme design and an information system may be established, tested and improved for the sake of the whole programme and future evaluations. Prior assessment of new programmes and projects in local development facilitates a "trial and error" approach to defining indicators, data collection methods, identification of key actors, and identifying and assessing expected results.

Even if the first selection of indicators or round of data collection turns out to be useless or ineffective, it may still be early enough in the programme cycle to adapt the chosen variables or instruments. All this is what makes an honest prior assessment so valuable – if it leads to reasonable changes and improvements in programme management and monitoring techniques.

Key actors

Aside from the technical staff in charge of the programme or policy, other key players in setting up an information system are the **implementing partners**. Their opinions with regard to the implementation of the programme and monitoring of activities will, ideally, be closely linked to those of the technical staff.

Primary stakeholders, who are involved in the programming and planning process, such as representatives of target groups, environmental organisations, local or regional development agencies, business support providers and so on, should also be considered in the development of an information system, particularly in their role as potential contributors and/or targets for specific information during or after programme implementation.

While potentially contributing specific information on sectors or target groups (surveys, studies or data), they may request specific aspects or effects to be monitored as a way of assessing the relevance, effectiveness and impact of the development strategy from their sector, local or individual point of view. Primary stakeholders in particular will have a more realistic view of expected results and may help in the *ex ante* appraisal of programme objectives and desired outcomes.

Other stakeholders (related institutions, other sector departments, regional or local third-sector partners, research institutes, business organisations, universities, etc.) should be considered as potential information sources. At the same time, they may be interested in some of the issues arising from the policy, which would make them particularly interested in its impacts.

Besides the parties involved in the development strategy, it may be helpful to rely on **practical and technical support** in information system implementation, maintenance and updating (*i.e.* consultants, information and communications technology [ICT] specialists, database or software developers, social researchers, specialists in statistics, evaluators, etc.). One issue to be defined from the very beginning is who will actually do the data collection, processing and analysis. This could be done by the staff who are implementing the programme or by external technical staff – whether an independent evaluation unit or a consultant – or by a combination of both.

Key activities

Key information system establishment activities should also go hand in hand with development strategy planning and programming.

A situation analysis or baseline studies (socio-economic analyses, pre-assessment, SWOT [strengths, weaknesses, opportunities and threats] analyses, etc.) will provide a detailed review of regional and local needs, according to different target groups, territorial units, sectors and/or policy fields. Such initial information should clearly influence the design of a local development strategy.

The following points should be considered, not only for programme management reasons, but also for the sake of a well-functioning information system:

- Identifying primary and secondary **stakeholders**.
- Determining the available **budget and other resources** (not only for implementing measures, but also for monitoring and evaluation).

- Planning the **time horizon** of the development strategy (implementation) and expected results and impacts. If focused on results, monitoring and evaluation should be continued after the end of implementation to detect and react to the observation and analysis of results (or the lack of results). **Milestones and key events** (meetings, data collection deadlines, annual report dates, evaluation deadlines, etc.) should be planned from the beginning and in accordance with the overall process of planning of future development strategies.
- Defining the **goals, objectives, purposes and activities** of the local development strategy, including the definition of performance questions and indicators. One useful technique is to classify the objectives of a development strategy hierarchically, linking each specific objective to its global objective (*e.g.* through an objective tree), thus making the overall intervention logic explicit.

Setting up an information system requires other activities, which depend on the final use to which the information collected should be put. Data is never collected as a means in itself, but rather as a basis for some further analysis, progress report or evaluation.

The character and function of this future use will determine, among other things, data requirements, data collection methods, the organisation of the information, deadlines, technical support requirements and the relation between quantitative and qualitative data. All these details should be clarified at the pre-assessment stage in a **conceptual mapping or evaluation matrix** (Table 6.1).

An evaluation matrix helps you to define what you want to know about your development strategy, in particular its relevance, effectiveness, efficiency, impact and sustainability.

For each of the **performance questions** you want to answer with your monitoring data, you should also define the quantitative and qualitative **indicators** you require; the **sources of information, data collecting methods**; as well as the **possible problems or limitations** that will need to be considered.

Setting up a conceptual framework for future information and evaluation needs is an **important feature of the prior assessment** of a local economic development strategy. Although not all of the details are already known or solved, it obliges technical staff and politicians to think about realistic information needs in a given context (and budget). Possible constraints may be accepted at this early stage or further resources could be dedicated to data gathering or analysis activities.

Table 6.1. **Two examples of a conceptual matrix for an information system**

Performance question and related targets	Information needs and indicators	Baseline information and status n	Data gathering: methods, frequency, limitations, responsibilities	Planning and resources: need for external experts	Information use: analysis, feedback, reporting, change management
1. Example: GOAL: Creation of new jobs and income generation through an improved entrepreneurial climate and more business activity.					
How did the local business culture change? 30% increase in business creation in programme lifetime.	Changes over time in % of total businesses created. Possible reasons for changes (other than the programme).	Total number and average annual change in % of local business creation figures.	Local commercial register statistics, new entrepreneur surveys. Monthly. Project technical staff will collect data.	Organise with local administrative staff at Register Bureau. Invite an expert for survey implementation and analysis.	Feedback and final report with data. At the end of the year, hold workshop to present findings and discuss programme results.
2. Example: GOAL: Better child nutrition and education, offering daily school breakfasts with balanced diets.					
Did the school breakfasts have any impact on children's health and malnutrition? 50% reduction of malnutrition among school children.	Did the school breakfasts have any impact on children's health and malnutrition? 50% reduction of malnutrition among school children.	Did the school breakfasts have any impact on children's health and malnutrition? 50% reduction of malnutrition among school children.	Did the school breakfasts have any impact on children's health and malnutrition? 50% reduction of malnutrition among school children.	Did the school breakfasts have any impact on children's health and malnutrition? 50% reduction of malnutrition among school children.	Did the school breakfasts have any impact on children's health and malnutrition? 50% reduction of malnutrition among school children.

Technical support

The setting up of a new information system may require important technical activities, which may, in turn, require the support of external experts and specialists.

It may be the case that the programme or policy for which the information system is being designed is so complex that monitoring may only be done using a computer system. This has been observed in some European Union countries with relation to the financial management of the European Structural Funds.

Once the need for such a monitoring system is confirmed, if the prior assessment has detected the need for data linked to the operations the computer system is to control, it may be technically feasible for it to be set up in such a way as to supervise and monitor more qualitative, strategic features of the policies and programmes involved (Box 6.1).

Box 6.1. **Example of an information and policy monitoring system: the National Agency for Regional Development, Slovenia**

One case of a complex policy monitoring system arose in Slovenia, where in order to support all the necessary activities relating to the country's economic development, the National Agency for Regional Development (NARD) proposed building an information system, the centre being a data warehouse that would be fed directly and systematically with data from different sources. This would mean that centralised implementation of contents supervision of all programmes and sub-programmes would be available in one place.

The first stage aimed to monitor territorial objectives. Data or indicators of different territories were taken directly from public databases (Statistics Office, Tax Agency, Employment Office, etc.) and fed into the data warehouse. In the NARD database, such data would be the basis for fulfilling information needs of NARD users or employees in a multidimensional form (Online Analytical Processing). Thus, the people responsible would be able to get regular reports on the state of projects, territories, etc. so as to monitor the achievement of objectives, analyse deviations from the projects and conduct research into the reasons. Later, it is intended to include both financial and physical data on implementing projects, sub-programmes, main programmes, priorities and finally programmes and strategies.

It is often more useful to start with a less technical information system that can be used in random assessment reports, progress control and evaluations, rather than creating cemeteries of useless data. This is usually the case of small-scale or local strategies. An information system may already be helpful with complete data files in simple databases or balance sheets, as well as complete sets of annual statistical reports on a given region or municipality.

It is vital to be realistic about information requirements in terms of the availability and validity of suggested variables. It is also important to have an awareness of the technical capacity required to launch complex information systems.

In many cases variables are not available at a sufficiently disaggregated level. For some variables the national statistical authority does not undertake data gathering at the local or regional level. It might then be necessary to define specific information systems to collect the information needed at the required territorial detail.

In other cases some variables may be available, but they are not available over a sufficient length of time to feed sophisticated analytical models. In such cases, a simple evaluation approach is needed in order to obtain results with a limited number of variables.

Finally, even where series of more sophisticated variables are available, it is helpful to carry out a prior assessment of the derived cost/benefit ratio involved in starting up an econometric or other, potentially overly sophisticated, system. This may avoid excessively high costs or major problems that could result in losing interest as policy application generates increasingly diversified processes that are more difficult to reduce to a mathematical or computer model. Here, a prior assessment of the policy would enable a comparison of the value and practicality of the selected variables, and to verify whether the method used for their analysis is suited to the evaluation of the programmes and policies under consideration.

Another aspect to be considered is how to overcome problems arising when it is not possible to obtain some of the data – or when part of it is missing – to be included in the information system.

In this case we have to use a range of techniques, such as completing the time series by analogy with developments in geographically more extensive zones, to using qualitative information to substitute quantitative data. Any results obtained this way would have to be carefully analysed so as to assess their coherence with the general conclusions drawn from the rest of the data. Any contradiction would mean analysing the reasons in detail, as the contradiction may be due to the fact that the evolution was in effect different or proved largely irrelevant. Ultimately, it may be necessary to change the interim or final conclusions to make them coherent with the global analysis framework.

What kind of data is needed?

Specific information needs should be defined in line with the foreseen hierarchy of development strategy objectives, since the main reason for collecting data in the first place is to answer specific questions related to activities, outputs, and overall results:

- Can planned activities be completed on time and with the resources available? How many partners are required, and who?
- What direct tangible products or services could the projects deliver as a result of activities?
- How would this affect target groups or the target sector? What are the potential effects of projects and activities?

- To what extent might the strategy contribute to longer-term goals? Can we define a clear and attributable relationship between activities, results and the changes in the overall (sector, local) regional socio-economic situation?

Considering the future use of the information system defined as a result of these considerations, we need to remember that when information is collected for assessment, evaluation and related improvements in programme management and implementation as well as progress control, then data is not the only important feature.

For example, why a project failed or was successful, whether the effects are sustainable or not, and what has been learned from strategy implementation for the future, the reasons are also important. In this case, analysis and interpretation of raw data is necessary and should be carried out in the form of mid-term or *ex post* evaluation or impact assessments.

For prior assessment, the gathering of baseline information and the overall design of information, monitoring and evaluation needs are the key aspects.

Monitoring data – the use of performance questions and indicators

To define more clearly what kind of information is needed, two tools are used in information and monitoring systems: performance questions and indicators. **Performance questions** help to make programme and project objectives operational and translate them into specific information needs.

As a crucial tool for monitoring and information handling, **indicators** should therefore not be listed in direct relation to programme objectives and goals (one to one), but as an attempt to answer specific performance questions. Specific information needs should be highlighted, even if a single quantitative indicator cannot describe them.

For example, if an objective of a given strategy is the "**development of businesses through the creation of a network of rural business incubators**", performance questions could help to break down and make operative the overall objective of "business development" as set out in Table 6.2.

As Figure 6.1 shows, indicators can be classified as baseline indicators, output indicators and result indicators.

Table 6.2. **Performance questions and indicators**

Performance questions	Indicators
How will the programme influence the number of existing firms?	Number of registered firms
How will the programme influence the region's sector structure; will firms emerge and consolidate in new (technology-based) sectors?	Number of registered firms per sector In-depth analysis of new (technology) sectors
Are the effects sustainable in time?	Mortality rate of newly created firms, changes over time (2-5 years)
What external factors have influenced any changes?	Analysis of external factors for business creation and overall economic climate

Figure 6.1. **Use of indicators in local development strategy management**

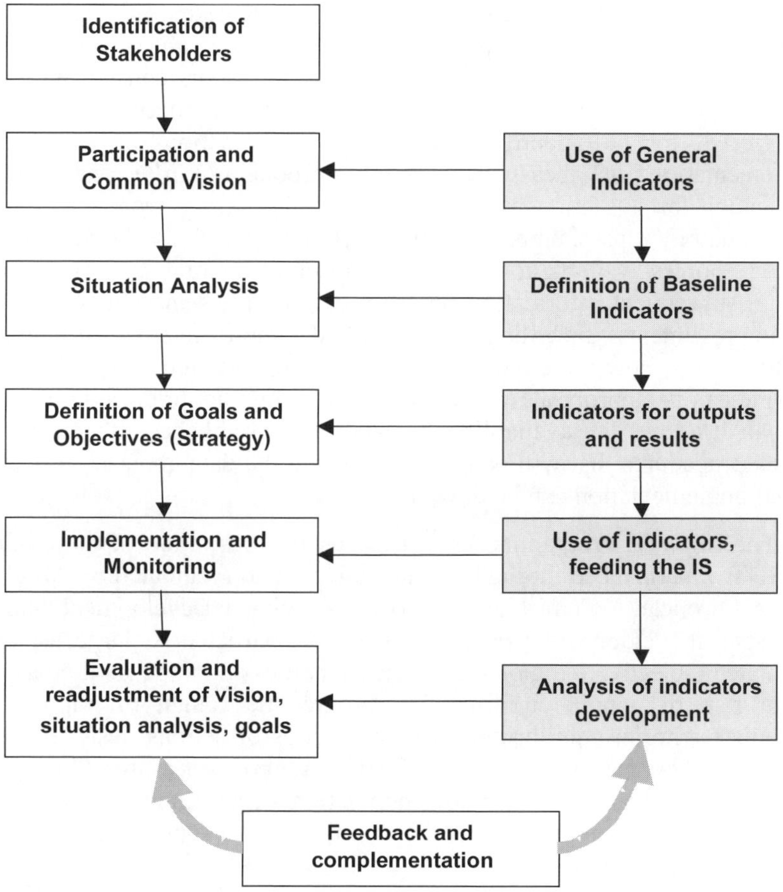

Impact and result indicators normally correspond to baseline indicators. Both try to show the overall socio-economic situation in a given local or regional context. By comparing a baseline (a time unit before project start or at the beginning of the strategy implementation) and the final situation (at n = programme end or at n+1, n+2, n+n), the impact of a strategy should become visible. However, given the limited size and budget of some strategies, as well as the importance of external factors (macro-economic evolution, crises), it is not always possible to detect relevant or attributable changes in baseline indicators. Quantitative, "easy-to-measure" indicators are particularly useful for describing programme activities and direct outputs (products, services delivered). To monitor results and effects, as well as meet specific information needs, qualitative indicators and in-depth information should be used to complement quantitative data.

It is precisely in the definition of these indicators where the information system can most clearly benefit from the prior assessment process. After an assessment, if suitable macro- or meso-economic statistical variables for measuring the impact of the policy to be implemented are shown not to be available, then we will need to define impact indicators consequent on the measures to be put into practice. At the same time, the necessary resources will need to be identified to collect information on the actual implementation of measures, *e.g.* by introducing in investment aid application forms sections requesting information on the type of enterprise, the technology it uses, employee skill levels, etc. It will also be necessary to make resources available for collecting impact information, *e.g.* by requiring certain subsequent information before providing assistance, including data on improvements in billing, jobs created, improvements in employee qualifications, how the export market has developed and so on. To define the indicators appropriately, the help given by the prior assessment is crucial. It allows the availability of data to be established. If not, internal policy procedures that will enable us to obtain the data about the effects of actual implementation can be developed.

The LEGITE Programme provides a useful illustration of these points. LEGITE was financed through an Innovative Action regulated by Article 10 of the European Commission's European Regional Development Fund in the Spanish region of *Castilla y León*, a particularly large, sparsely populated Objective 1 region with industrial cities and huge rural areas with major risk of population drift. The programme sought to improve the region's territorial equilibrium through a series of actions designed to get technology improvement and innovation support measures through to peripheral rural areas, where low population density and the scarcity of businesses made it impossible to generate the kind of support infrastructures available in urban zones.

It was clear from the outset that major problems would be encountered in the evaluation of the programme's impact. In the first place, the programme's macro-economic impact was going to be very limited, largely because the total number of beneficiary businesses would represent a small percentage of the total number of enterprises in the region. Furthermore, its effect on the economy as a whole would only really become clear several years after the programme had ended. Statistics available in Spain also made it impossible to follow the evolution of zones where the programme was to be implemented, as it involved territorial units such as municipalities or even smaller, for which there are no statistics (much less business statistics), and where they did exist, were not readily available.

The regional authorities were advised to develop a series of *ad hoc* indicators allowing them to monitor LEGITE's impact on businesses and territories later. This led to the definition of an information system based on micro- and meso-economic variables that were relevant to the objectives set. The variables were defined realistically, as the idea was to make then genuinely operational, reasonable to obtain in terms of resources and available readily. The indicator system defined specifically for LEGITE is shown in Table 6.3.

Quality of indicators

The quality of indicators and the appropriate selection of quantitative, qualitative and/or descriptive information needs contribute considerably to the overall quality and usefulness of the information system.

Several guidelines are available that help to define valuable and useful indicators. The SMART methodology is perhaps the best known guideline, used by many evaluators and monitoring and evaluation managers. SMART means that indicators should be specific, measurable, achievable, realistic and time-bound.

Other guides stress the importance of the validity, reliability and relevance of the indicators, and that their use is reasonable in terms of cost and the time needed for them to be processed.

It should also be noted that more indicators do not automatically imply a better information system. To be manageable and easy to use, and owing to common restrictions of resources and budget, the number of indicators should be limited and the information system should focus on the "necessary" information.

Table 6.3. **LEGITE innovative action *Castilla y León* - summary of indicators**
(proposed pre-implementation)

Indicators for monitoring	
Action 1: Demand boost	• Number of diagnoses performed • Number of technology audits • Number of action plans carried out • Number of conferences and seminars • Qualified executive staff trained • External specialists identified, selected and trained • Handbook and other material prepared • Evolution of budgeted expenses • Number of enterprises contacted
Action 2: Technology watch forecast and intelligence	• Number of sector or cluster forums started up • Number of action plans at technology centres • Number of technology centre internationalisation projects • Increase in international projects where technology centres partner with regional businesses • Number of businesses taking part in forums • Number of research projects started up • Reports and other material prepared • Evolution of budgeted expenses
Action 3: Excellence policy in digital content industry	• Number of businesses taking part in workshops • Number of university departments participating directly or indirectly in the action • Number of innovative projects for existing enterprises • Number of proposals for the creation of new enterprises • Number of new entrepreneurial projects • Evolution of the budgeted expenses
Action 4: Policy definition	• Number of international networks in which take part • Number of diffusion activities • Reports and handbooks elaborated • Evolution of the budgeted expenses
Indicators to measure global impacts and effects of the LEGITE Programme	
Changes in business opinions about innovation and valuation of the programme in particular New entrepreneurial attitudes towards innovation Evolution of budget execution as compared to the one programmed (analysis of diversion) Number of participant small and medium-sized enterprises (SMEs) in the actions Number of SMEs assisted by the action Increases in business investment in innovation in targeted sectors Quantitative increase and changes in business use of Internet (e-business and e-commerce)	

Indicators to be used should be defined **before** data collection starts. That means in or even before the prior assessment. When different partners and stakeholders are involved in data gathering, a clear and agreed definition for the particular information system should be in place to avoid misunderstandings, errors in data collection and, finally, useless data records and lack of comparability.

In the prior assessment process all these aspects may be reviewed as regards the information system, as you can verify in practice if, and how, data can be obtained, and if such data can be used to provide results relevant to what the programme is designed to achieve.

Table 6.4 is an example of a comprehensive indicator sheet that establishes an ensemble of categories for a given indicator, relating in this case to a new business creation policy.

Table 6.4. **Indicator sheet**

Definition/name:	Business development (new firms)
Purpose (why are we measuring it?):	To monitor the creation of business activity in a rural area
Priority:	Core
Numerator:	Number of newly registered firms in the region in one year
Denominator:	All registered firms
Measurement tools:	Business Register at the Chamber of Commerce
Timeframe	2000-05
What it measures:	The indicator tracks the creation of new businesses in the region.
How to measure it:	The total number of newly registered firms (in one year) over the last five years will be collected, as well as the total number of registered firms.
Strengths and limitations:	The indicator shows the objective figure of new firms in the area. This is a good indicator to measure the effects of the support for new business activities within our programme. However, business creation may well depend on other external factors (macro-economic climate, bank loans, existence of venture capital) that we have not been able to influence so far. In addition, business growth may be cyclical.
Analysis and interpretation:	To be able to interpret the raw data, we will calculate the yearly growth rate for the last five years (in % of previous year). The indicator can be compared to the national average and to other regions of comparable size in order to detect overall developments. Interviews with new entrepreneurs should be conducted to detect other factors that influenced the recent development. The indicator should be related to the mortality of firms and an overall business growth rate should be established. This will help to interpret the figures and to connect them with the overall impact of our programme (development of the regional economy).

One activity may require different types of indicators (activity, output, result). This refers to the difference between addressing the **level** (pure number or unit), the **level of change** (absolute change or change rate in percent, evolution over time), the **extent** of an activity or coverage (in percent of a whole or a specific population group), the **relevance** within a wider context (percent participation in a regional or national average or total figure, index calculation). The type of indicator that best responds to actual information needs and what this means for the data-gathering process (*e.g.* the need for national figures or statistical time series) should be clear from the beginning.

The importance of baseline data

Creating sufficient baseline data is a crucial activity. It is impossible to assess the value and impact of a programme or project activity only by output or result indicators. To be useful, monitoring data must be related to the wider local and programme framework. The following information should be available from the beginning:

- The situation (socio-economic, of target groups, external conditions) before implementation of the strategy.
- The strategy and its operational plan (timeline, milestones, foreseen activities, expected results, financial resources and budget, other resources, management and monitoring and evaluation activities).

Changes in the overall or a specific local socio-economic situation, which, intended or not, may have been caused by a programme and its activities, can only be observed, measured and adequately analysed when comparable data with regard to the previous situation exists in the framework of an information system. In addition, information in the shape of indicators should be available on activities planned, the results expected and resources to be used. In particular, the effectiveness and efficiency of a given programme can only be determined and assessed if relevant information exists on the original programme planning. In this context it is important to stress that changes in programme planning during the programme implementation phase are easier to cope with when possible modifications regarding performance questions, expected results, indicators to be used, etc. are introduced in an updated version of programme design or an adapted version of prior assessment. Gathering baseline information involves two different forms of studies:

- A **situation analysis**, which should already have been produced as part of the programme design.
- A **baseline survey** (including definition of information needs and indicators), which is undertaken after programme design has been completed.

A situation analysis is more open-ended in terms of the themes and questions analysed (such as the problems and needs of stakeholders, institutional setting, organisational links, cultural background, external variables which may influence programme results), while a baseline survey normally only includes data and specific indicators needed to make impact-related comparisons. Situation analysis normally requires qualitative methods (in-depth studies, case studies, focus groups, face-to-face interviews, observation) to detect relevant information, whereas baseline surveys refer mostly to the gathering of quantitative, statistical or official survey data.

Practically every local development strategy, programme or project is based on a formal or informal situation analysis, which detects the need to act in the first place (a development problem, desire for improvement, etc.). To make informal or popular knowledge usable for prior assessment and any future evaluations, informal information should be **formalised** or at least written down (as a case study, a narration, etc.) and stored as part of the baseline information of the development programme. Obviously, qualitative information obtained from the situation analysis could and should be used during and after programme implementation, even if it cannot be presented by means of quantitative and objective indicators. The opinions of stakeholders involved, a description of the state of the art and the review of habits, regular practices and routines may be compared in another round of focus groups, interviews, case studies or observations during an intermediate or final evaluation as a means of detecting tangible changes associated with the programme. Occasionally, it may be difficult to carry out comprehensive baseline studies prior to the implementation of a programme and its activities. As alternatives to the elaboration of new baseline studies, information systems could be built on:

- Existing **qualitative information** of the situation analysis as a starting point for future comparisons: this approach has just been presented. It facilitates some insight into the tangible and intangible impacts of a programme. However, the information will be mostly testimonial and subjective and should be complemented with objective data as soon as possible during programme implementation.
- **Rolling baselines** as a middle-ground option between undertaking a baseline or a total retrospective assessment in the future: as resources sometimes only become available as programmes are implemented, technical staff will need to launch activities together, and collect baseline data and formalise informal knowledge as fast as possible. In this situation, programme activities must be combined with a steady effort to gather baseline data and to complete the baseline data during the programme lifetime, ideally until the mid-term evaluation. Although

the baseline information may in this case relate to several different "baselines", it will provide an overview of the situation before programme implementation or impact generation.

- The use of **existing research documentation** that does not require field data collection: earlier programmes and projects have often been implemented or at least research has been conducted in the field where baseline information on socio-economic indicators is necessary. This information may be used, even if it does not reflect the "initial" situation of the new project, but the "final" situation of a programme that concluded some 18 months ago. Additional data might be available in research reports, doctoral theses, thematic studies or other sources, which are not available on administration bookshelves, but can be found on the Internet, at the local university, at environmental organisations or non-governmental organisations, etc.

How to find and collect monitoring data

Apart from the data obtained in the actual implementation of the programme (forms, surveys, opinion of programme management, etc.), you may use different and complementary social research methods to find and collect monitoring data. The selection of adequate methods is limited in many cases by restrictions of time, budget and/or other resources. However, some general rules should be established and followed in order to guarantee data objectivity and comparability.

Information sources

People and documents are the main sources of information. Although different sources of information will be exploited for different programmes and strategies, some sources should be considered in any case. Remember that certain sources only have a specific and limited knowledge of the programme, according to their particular perspective. For example, there is no point in asking programme managers about programme effects on particular target groups if they do not know about, or only have a largely biased view of, the real global impact of the programme. Below is a list of the most relevant information sources that are normally easiest to find and their particular knowledge fields:

- Programme management → operational information, financial management, payments, funding structure, expected results, equipment and staff management, etc.

- Implementing partners or bodies (public, private, other) → operational information and financial management of specific activities, project implementation, problems and relevant changes during implementation.
- Participants in supported activities and schemes (during activity but also tracking of benefits after implementation, six months, one year, two years) → implementation and operational management of specific activities, relevance of activities and projects, outputs, results and impacts on their specific situation.
- Beneficiaries (direct and indirect) or representatives of target groups (associations, foundations, NGOs, etc.) → relevance of programme and specific activities, outcomes and impacts of global programme and its activities, sustainability.
- General stakeholders and representatives of cross-cutting or horizontal issues (environmental organisations, ethnic minorities, female or migrant associations, children's organisations, etc.) → relevance of programme and specific activities, integration of horizontal and cross-cutting issues in programme design and implementation, outcomes and impacts of global programme and its activities from a particular perspective.
- Existing information and data-gathering systems (national and regional statistical systems from the government or other agencies) → socio-economic situation, context and baseline indicators, evolution of specific and thematic issues, impacts of global programme and its activities.

Useful data collection methods

For prior assessment, quantitative methods (for the baseline survey) should be combined with qualitative methods (as part of the situation analysis) to get the whole picture of the *ex ante* situation. Qualitative methods such as face-to-face interviews, focus groups and case studies may be time-consuming and provide few clear-cut, measurable indicators. However, they are essential at the beginning of a programme as a basis for future interpretations of outcomes and results and to detect possible intangible impacts on the beneficiary groups. According to the requirements on data, the focus will either be on quantitative indicators, qualitative (additional) information, background and expert information, or on general observations of actions and stakeholder interactions. The most important data collection methods would include:

- Methods for collecting primary data (interviews, surveys, observation, focus groups, etc.).

- Methods for collecting secondary data (review of documents and operational or financial information, analysis of statistics and other information, use of previous or related evaluations, impact assessments or monitoring reports, etc.).
- Methods for collecting spatial information or linking data with territorial units (geographic information systems, mapping, photographs and videos).
- Methods for collecting expert opinions and qualitative background information (expert panels, Delphi rounds, case studies, etc.).

Some of the most common data collection methods, and their specific implications, are shown in Table 6.5.

Table 6.5. **Some of the most common data collection methods**

Questionnaire survey	A written or electronic version of the questionnaire. Details of institutions and persons to whom the questionnaire will be sent, by mail or e-mail. The selected people will or will not return the questionnaire. Especially suited to covering a large population and satisfying a need for statistical data in a given area. **Disadvantages**: You need to test the questionnaire before sending it. The rate of return is normally low without reminders by mail or telephone. There is little room for explanations, qualitative answers, comments or second questions. Very time-consuming.
Face-to-face interview	This method requires personal interaction. You will need an interview guideline with open or closed (yes/no) questions and an interviewer with experience in this technique, who will register and codify the answers for further analysis. **Disadvantages**: It requires experienced interviewers. All interviewers should be trained specifically to obtain comparable and objective results. Codification of answers may lead to a loss of qualitative information or too much information.
Telephone interview	This is a personal interview made by telephone. Less qualitative information will be obtained than in a face-to-face interview, but it is less time-consuming. Suited for closed questions and if the group of people you want to interview is geographically dispersed. **Disadvantages**: The attention of the interviewee will descend after a certain time. There is a lack of personal interaction and rapport, which could influence the level of trust and honest answers.
Group techniques (group interview, workshop, focus group)	This requires discussion in small groups (normally 7-12 people) with similar characteristics or representing a particular stakeholder group. You will need an experienced group facilitator to guide the group and the discussion, as well as someone to write down the comments. **Disadvantages**: This requires good preparation, the availability of a whole group and an expert in group techniques. It will be difficult to obtain quantitative information. Some members of the group might not feel free to speak.
Document review	You need the documents, reports or evaluations in a written or electronic form to review them thoroughly. Information needs to be summarised, classified and made usable for further analysis. Especially valuable if you need background data or a historic perspective regarding a particular problem, region, etc. **Disadvantages**: The information might be outdated, unorganised, or not objective. You might need to read up and do scientific research. The use of various sources might include the risk of mix and comparing statistics or data that are not comparable.

In cases where too little or no quantitative data is available, the collection of data and the creation of a local/regional information system in a specific field (business environment, environmental situation, health or education situation, infrastructure, etc.) could, in itself, be part of the local development programme. An information system might be included as a specific ongoing programme line (monitoring and evaluation system) or might be built up as an initial step within the overall programme development.

If little or no resources can be dedicated to an external study for the collection and preparation of baseline information during a prior assessment, internships and doctoral students may offer valuable support, being grateful for the practical experience.

What to do with all the data

The final step in completing an information system is the preparation of the raw data and its transformation into valuable and useful information.

How to turn monitoring data into useful information – storage, classification and updating

Data can be maintained over a relevant time period. While keeping it available for use in progress reporting and evaluation, the conditions and necessary requirements for data storage, classification and updating need to be considered at the very start of the information system setup.

Data storage involves the consideration of sufficient storage place, either physical (storage rooms) or virtual (adequate software, computer memory capacity). Control and auditing obligations make it increasingly important to store operational data, as well as contracts and expenditure data, for at least ten years.

Classification of data is a relevant issue if large amounts of data need to be prepared for future use. Each information system should find its own way of classifying data according to information requirements (per project, programme line, target group, type of activity, etc.). Modern databases and specific information system software increasingly permits automatic programme data classification and storage.

Aggregation of data regarding single project activities, locations or time periods may be another necessary step in data preparation. Data storage and treatment systems should be able to aggregate and summarise data according to information needs.

Regular **updating** is necessary not only for the data to be collected, but also for the particular information needs of the stakeholders involved and the selection and definition of useful indicators and data collection methods.

Use of monitoring information

Information systems fulfil their function only if they offer useful information for monitoring, control, assessment and evaluation purposes. They complete their commitment if available data and information is finally used.

The active and recommendable use of monitoring information in the context of local development strategies includes two steps:

1. The use of raw monitoring information in the phases of project and programme evaluation, revision of strategies or final assessment of activities.
2. The use of evaluation and assessment reports (where monitoring data has been interpreted as well as complemented and cross-checked with other types of information) for learning purposes (revising strategies, adapting or developing new projects or readjusting schemes and measures), as well as for accountability (the presentation of outputs, outcomes, results and impacts).

Conclusions

Information systems are one of the key elements of a local development strategy monitoring and evaluation system. Setting up of a useful and functional information system requires proper understanding of programme development and evaluation processes. At first sight, "information system" is a general management term that must be adapted to the context of a specific local or regional development strategy that needs to be monitored and assessed. It may involve files of written data on programme activities and beneficiary and target group surveys, but it will also require an integrated software package and modern technical support (databases, ICT) used in programme implementation by all project managers and overall programme management. Professional information systems need technical support, related to the requirements for data collection, data storage and classification. However, it may be more important to create a feasible and useful information system that facilitates basic data and conclusions on project activities, outputs and results, rather than having a comprehensive, but overly complex data storage system in place, without the capacity to analyse or use the data correctly.

Information Systems – Summary of Do's and Don'ts

Do's

- Start with simple, common sense approaches.
- Define performance questions for each of your programme objectives and plan future monitoring and evaluation activities.
- Use a limited number of key indicators with realistic possibilities of obtaining updated data.
- Define the baseline situation through indicators and qualitative information.
- Define a time horizon for impact evaluation and analysis in line with the time it takes to produce socio-economic impacts and to change habits and mindsets.

Don'ts

- Don't try to cover everything by generating a complex, ultimately unusable system.
- Don't define a system that is based on unavailable, inexistent or useless data.
- Don't forget the real objectives of policy makers and stakeholders.

Bibliography

African Development Bank (2003), *Guidelines and Methodologies for Evaluation,* prepared by the Operations Evaluation Department (OPEV) of the African Development Bank.

African Development Bank (2004), *Efficacy and Efficiency of Monitoring-Evaluation Systems (MES) for Projects Financed by the Bank Group*, prepared by the Operations Evaluation Department (OPEV) of the African Development Bank. Asian Development Bank (2006), *Guidelines for the Preparation of Country Assistance Program Evaluation Reports*, Operations Evaluation Department (OED) of the Asian Development Bank.

Asian Development Bank (2006), *Impact Evaluation Methodological and Operational Issues*, Economic Analysis and Operations Support Division and Economics and Research Department of the Asian Development Bank.

Asian Development Bank (2006), *Guidelines for Preparing Performance Evaluation Reports for Public Sector Operations*, www.adb.org/Documents/Guidelines/Evaluation/PPER-PSO/default.asp.

Baker, J.L. (2000), *Evaluating the Impact of Development Projects on Poverty: A Handbook for Practitioners*, World Bank Publications, Washington, DC.

Banks, R. (2000), "*Ex Ante* Evaluations: Strengths, Weaknesses and Opportunities", paper prepared for the European Commission's Edinburgh Conference, "Evaluation for Quality", 4th European Conference on Evaluation of the Structural Funds, Edinburgh, 18-19 September 2000.

Bardach, E. (2005), *A Practical Guide for Policy Analysis: The Eightfold Path to More Effective Problem Solving*, Chatham House Publishers, New York.

Bemelmans-Videc, M.L., R.C. Rist and E. Vedung (1998), *Carrots, Sticks and Sermons: Policy Instruments and Their Evaluation*, Transaction Publishers, New Jersey.

Blazek, J. and J. Vozab (2003), "Forming Evaluation Capacity and Culture in the Czech Republic: Experience with the First Set of *Ex Ante* Evaluations of Programming Documents (with Special Focus on Evaluation of UNDP)", paper presented at the 5th European Conference on Evaluation of the Structural Funds, Budapest, 26-27 June 2003, http://europa.eu.int/comm/regional_policy/sources/docconf/budapeval/work/blazek.doc.

Boyle, R. and D. Lemaire (1999), *Building Effective Evaluation Capacity: Lessons from Practice*, Transaction Publishers, New Jersey.

Bozeman, B. and J. Melkers (1993), *Evaluating R&D Impacts: Methods and Practice*, Springer, New York.

Bradley, J., J. Zaleski and P. Zuber (2003), *The Role of* Ex Ante *Evaluation in CEE National Development Planning*, Springer, New York, http://europa.eu.int/comm/regional_policy/sources/docconf/budapeval/work/bradley.doc.

Chacon-Moscos, S., *et al.* (2002), *A Mutual Catalytic Model of Formative Evaluation: The Interdependent Roles of Evaluators and Local Programme Practitioners*, Sage Publications, London.

Charities Evaluation Services (CES) (2005), "First Steps in Monitoring and Evaluation", London, www.ces-vol.org.uk/downloads/firstmande-15-21.pdf.

Chelimsky, E. and W.R. Shadish (1997), *Evaluation for the 21st Century: A Handbook,* Sage Publications, London.

Clarke, A. (1999), *Evaluation Research: An Introduction to Principles, Methods and Practice*, Sage Publications, London.

Commission of the European Communities (2005), "Impact Assessment and *Ex Ante* Evaluation", COM(2005)119final, www.avcr.cz/data/vav/vav-eu/SEK2005_0430_EN_exante.pdf.

Dartiguepeyrou, C., *et al.* (2005), "A Dynamic Framework for *Ex Ante* Evaluation and Assessment of New is Policies", prepared for the European Commission, Directorate-General Information Society.

DTI (Department of Trade and Industry) (1999), "Guidance on Preparing Evaluation Plans", ES Central Evaluation Team, DTI, London.

European Commission (no date), "Evaluating EU Activities: A Practical Guide for the Commission Services", Evaluation Guides, EC, Brussels, http://ec.europa.eu/budget/library/publications/financial_pub/eval_activities_en.pdf.

European Commission (no date), "Good Practice Guidelines for the Management of the Evaluation Functions", Evaluation Guides, EC, Brussels, http://ec.europa.eu/dgs/information_society/evaluation/data/pdf/lib_master/sec2000_1051_strengthening_eval.pdf.

European Commission (2000), "The *Ex Ante* Evaluation of the Structural Funds Interventions", Methodological Working Papers No. 2, EC, Brussels, http://europa.eu.int/comm/regional_policy/sources/docoffic/working/doc/exante_en.pdf.

European Commission (2000), "Indicators for Monitoring and Evaluation: An Indicative Methodology", Methodological Working Papers, No. 3, Directorate-General XVI, Regional Policy and Cohesion, EC, Brussels.

European Commission (2000), "Structural Funds 2000-2006: *Ex Ante* Evaluation and Indicators for INTERREG III (Strands A & B)", Methodological Working Papers, No. 7, Directorate-General Regional Policy, EC, Brussels.

European Commission (2001), "*Ex Ante* Evaluation: A Practical Guide for Preparing Proposals for Expenditure Programmes", Directorate-General Budget, EC, Brussels.

European Commission (2004), "Annual Evaluation Review 2003: Overview of the Commission's Evaluation Activities and Main Evaluation Findings", Commission Staff Working Paper, SEC 662, Directorate-General Budget, EC, Brussels.

European Commission (2005), "Draft Working Paper on *Ex Ante* Evaluation", Methodological Working Papers, Directorate-General Regional Policy, EC, Brussels.

European Commission (2006), "Indicative Guidelines on Evaluation Methods: *Ex Ante* Evaluation", Methodological Working Papers, No. 1, Directorate-General Regional Policy, EC, Brussels.

European Commission (2006), "Indicative Guidelines on Evaluation Methods: Monitoring and Evaluation Indicators", Methodological Working Papers, No. 2, Directorate-General Regional Policy, EC, Brussels.

European Commission (2006), "Guidance on the Methodology for Carrying Out Cost-Benefit Analysis", Methodological Working Papers, No. 4, Directorate-General Regional Policy, EC, Brussels.

European Commission (2006), "Indicative Guidelines on Evaluation Methods: Evaluation during the Programming Period", Methodological Working Papers, No. 5, Directorate-General Regional Policy, EC, Brussels.

European Commission (2007), "Sourcebook on Sound Planning of ESF Programmes", EC, Brussels, www.esfsourcebook.eu.

EPRC and Fraser of Allander (2000), "Methodologies Used in the Evaluation of the Effectiveness of European Structural Funds: Comparative Assessment", Final Report to the Scottish Executive, European Policies Research Centre and the Fraser of Allander Institute, University of Strathclyde, Glasgow.

Evalsed and European Commission (2003), "The Guide to the Evaluation of Socio-Economic Development", Directorate-General Regional Policy, EC, Brussels, http://ec.europa.eu/regional_policy/sources/docgener/evaluation/evalsed/guide/index_en.htm.

Evalsed and European Commission (2003), "The Resource for the Evaluation of Socio-Economic Development", Directorate-General Regional Policy EC, Brussels, http://ec.europa.eu/regional_policy/sources/docgener/evaluation/evalsed/sourcebooks/index_en.htm.

Furubo, J.E, R.C. Rist and R. Sandahl (2002), *International Atlas of Evaluation*, Transaction Publishers, London.

HM Treasury (2002), "Appraisal and Evaluation in Central Government: Treasury Guidance", *The Green Book*, HM Treasury, London, www.hm-treasury.gov.uk/media/05553/Green_Book_03.pdf.

HM Treasury (2004), "Productivity in the UK 5: Benchmarking UK Productivity Performance: A Consultation on Productivity Indicators", HM Treasury, London, www.hm-treasury.gov.uk/consultations_and_legislation/productivity_indicators.

Ho, S.Y. (2003), *Evaluating British Urban Policy: Ideology, Conflict and Compromise*, Ashgate Publishing, Aldershot.

IFAD (International Fund for Agricultural Development) (2003), "Managing for Impact in Rural Development. A Guide for Project M&E", Section 4: Setting up the M&E System, The Office of Evaluation of the International Fund for Agricultural Development, Roma, www.ifad.org/evaluation/guide/index.htm.

Jaszczołt, K., T. Potkański and S. Alwasiak (2003), "Internal Project M&E System and Development of Evaluation Capacity: Experience of the World Bank-funded Rural Development Program", http://europa.eu.int/comm/regional_policy/sources/docconf/budapeval/work/jaszczolt.doc.

Mackay, K. (1998), *Public Sector Performance: The Critical Role of Evaluation*, World Bank Publications, Washington, DC.

Mackay, K. (1999), *Evaluation Capacity Development: A Diagnostic Guide and Action Framework,* World Bank Publications, Washington, DC.

Mairate, A. (2001), "Indicators for Monitoring and Evaluation, Conference on Decentralised Management of the Structural Funds (Objective 2)", http://europa.eu.int/comm/regional_policy/sources/docconf/manag2/maira_en.pdf.

ODPM (2003), "Assessing the Impacts of Spatial Interventions, Regeneration, Renewal and Regional Development Main Guidance", Interdepartmental Group on the EGRUP Review, Office of the Deputy Prime Minister, London.

OECD (2001), *Best Practices in Local Development*, OECD, Paris.

OECD (2002), *Glossary of Key Terms in Evaluation and Results Based Management,* Development Assistance Committee, OECD, Paris, www.oecd.org/dataoecd/29/21/2754804.pdf.

OECD (2003), *Entrepreneurship and Local Economic Development: Programme and Policy Recommendations*, OECD, Paris.

OECD (2004), *Evaluating Local Economic and Employment Development: How to Assess What Works among Programmes and Policies*, OECD, Paris.

OECD (2005), *Local Governance and the Drivers of Growth*, OECD, Paris.

OECD (2005), *Joint Evaluations: Recent Experiences, Lessons Learned and Options for the Future*, DAC Evaluation Network Working Paper, OECD, Paris, www.oecd.org/dataoecd/28/9/35353699.pdf.

OPRE (Office of Planning, Research and Evaluation) (2003), "The Program Manager's Guide to Evaluation", www.acf.hhs.gov/programs/opre/other_resrch/pm_guide_eval/reports/pmguide/pmguide_toc.html.

Owen, J.M. and P.J. Rogers (2006), *Program Evaluation: Forms and Approaches*, Guilford Press, United Kingdom.

Patton, C.V. and D.S. Sawicki (1986), *Basic Methods of Policy Analysis and Planning*, Prentice-Hall, New Jersey.

Patton, M.Q. (1997), *Utilization-Focused Evaluation,* 3rd edition, Sage Publications, London.

Pawson, R. (2006), *Evidence-Based Policy: A Realist Perspective*, Sage Publications, London.

Peters, C.C. and B. Warwick (1996), *The Handbook of Managed Futures: Performance, Evaluation and Analysis*, McGraw-Hill Trade, New York.

Prennushi, G., G. Rubio and K. Subbarao (2000), *Monitoring and Evaluation - In Sourcebook for Poverty Reduction Strategies*, World Bank Publications, Washington, DC.

Preskill, H. and R.T. Torres (1999), "Building Capacity for Organisational Learning Through Evaluative Inquiry", *Evaluation*, Vol. 5, No. 1, pp. 42-60, Sage Publications, London.

Preskill, H. and R.T. Torres (2000), "The Learning Dimension of Evaluation Use, New Directions for Evaluation", *New Directions for Evaluation*, No. 88, pp. 25-37, Sage Publications, London.

Puttaswamaiah, K. (1982), *Studies in Evaluation*, Oxford and IBH, New Delhi.

Rawlings, L. and J. Van Domelen (2004), *Evaluating Social Funds: A Cross-Country Analysis of Community Interventions*, World Bank Publications, Washington, DC.

Rist, R.C. and N. Stame (2006), *From Studies to Streams: Managing Evaluative Systems*, Transaction Publishers, New Jersey.

Romanainen, J. (2004), "Learning More from Evaluations: The Use of the Thematic Approach and Impact Modelling in Evaluating Public Support Measures", European Conference on Good Practice in Research Evaluation and Indicators, University of Galway, Ireland.

Rossi, P.H., H.E. Freeman and M.W. Lipsey (1999), *Evaluation: A Systematic Approach*, Sage Publications, London.

Rutman, L. (1977), *Evaluation Research Methods: A Basic Guide*, Sage Publications, London.

Tavistock Institute with GHK and IRS (2003), *The Evaluation of Socio-Economic Development: The Guide*, Tavistock Institute, London.

Torres, R., H. Preskill and M. Piontek (1996), *Evaluation Strategies for Communicating and Reporting: Enhancing Learning in Organizations*, Sage Publications, London.

Toulemonde, J. and T. Bjornkilde (2003), "Building Evaluation Capacity the Experience and Lesson in Member States and Acceding Countries", http://europa.eu.int/comm/regional_policy/sources/docconf/budapeval/work/toulemonde.doc.

UK Prime Minister's Strategy Unit (2000), "A Performance and Innovation Unit Report", Government Chief Social Researcher's Office, London, www.policyhub.gov.uk/docs/addingitup.pdf.

UK Prime Minister's Strategy Unit (2003), "Guidance Notes for Policy Evaluation and Analysis", Government Chief Social Researcher's Office, London, www.policyhub.gov.uk/downloads/Chapter_1.pdf.

UNDP (United Nations Development Programme) (2002), *Handbook on Monitoring and Evaluating for Development Results*, Evaluation Office, www.undp.org/eo/documents/HandBook/ME-HandBook.pdf.

UNDP and the World Bank (2000), *Evaluation Capacity Development in Asia*, World Bank Publications, Washington, DC.

Vedung, E. (1997), *Public Policy and Program Evaluation*, Transaction Publishers, New Jersey.

Weiss, C. (1999), "The Interface Between Evaluation and Public Policy", *Evaluation: The International Journal of Theory, Research, and Practice*, Graduate School of Education, Harvard, Boston, pp. 468–486.

Wholey, J.S. (1983), "Evaluation and Effective Public Management", *Public Productivity Review*, Vol. 7, No. 4, M.E. Sharpe, Boston.

Wholey, J.S, H.P. Hatry and K.E. Newcomer (2004), *Handbook of Practical Program Evaluation*, John Wiley & Sons, New Jersey.

Wollmann, H. (2003), *Evaluation in Public Sector Reform: Concepts and Practice in International Perspective*, Edward Elgar Publishing, UK.

World Bank (1994), "Building Evaluation Capacity", *Lessons and Practices*, No. 4, World Bank Publications, Washington, DC.

World Bank (1996), "Designing Project Monitoring and Evaluation", *Lessons and Practices*, No. 8, World Bank Publications, Washington, DC.

World Bank (1997), "Evaluating Development Outcomes: Methods for Judging Outcomes and Impacts", *Lessons and Practices*, No. 10, World Bank Publications, Washington, DC.

World Bank (1998), *Assessing Development Effectiveness: Evaluation in the World Bank and the International Finance Corporation*, World Bank Publications, Washington, DC.

World Bank (2004), *Monitoring and Evaluation (M&E): Some Tools, Methods and Approaches*, World Bank Publications, Washington, DC.

World Bank (2007), "How to Build M&E Systems to Support Better Government", Independent Evaluation Group, www.worldbank.org/ieg/ecd/docs/How_to_build_ME_gov.pdf

Zall Kusek, J. and R.C. Rist (2004), *Ten Steps to a Results-Based Monitoring and Evaluation System: A Handbook for Development Practitioners*, World Bank Publications, Washington, DC.

OECD PUBLICATIONS, 2, rue André-Pascal, 75775 PARIS CEDEX 16
PRINTED IN FRANCE
(84 2008 05 1 P) ISBN-978-92-64-04485-2 – No. 56201 2008